Moving

I could
put my roots down anywhere,
be there a bird.
Lacking a bird, a tree for potential.

No tree?
Well,
then any shrub.

I could make do
with plains of grasses
if I had known, or still might know
mountains.

Rivers I have loved,
but I could dream underground fountains
if I must.

Shrub, grasses, tree
and river failing,
I could live on rock,
knowing earth's cool history
cultivate lichens, harvest moss;

be ready in all places
to plant my body for time
to reap once more sweet earth, grass, shrub,
tree on plain, mountain,
for bird and all thousands of times again
again
dissolving into song.

Moving Gone Dancing

Publishing History for MOVING GONE DANCING

For first publication of the following poems, I gratefully acknowledge these journals and magazines.

Agnes Scott College Writers' Festival Collection, 1994: "By Whatever Degree of Sun"

Atlanta Review, Fall/Winter, 2003: "An Appalachian Woman Counts the Ways"

Casa Azul, April/May, 1998: "Had We Together Known Red Bougainvillea"; "Horacio, Por Favor"

Georgia Journal, Winter, 1992: "Modified"; Summer 1993: "Again This Summer"; Summer, 1994: "Lineage"

Habersham Review, Volume II, Number 1, Spring, 1993: "At Nasawaddox"; Volume III, Number 2: "On the Way to Port Matilda I, II"

Lights in the Mountains, North Carolina Writers' Network West, Anthology 2003: "Surveying Trillium"

Lucidity, Third Quarter, 1994: "Straight Shift"

Nimrod International Journal of Prose and Poetry, Volume 34, Number 2, Spring/Summer, 1991: "In Storage"; "Remainder"

The Chattahoochee Review, 1989-1990: "Wisteria"; 1991-1992: "Too Soon"; Spring, 1993, Volume XIII, Number 3: "Moving"; Volume XV, Number 1, Fall, 1993: "The Dahlia Man"; Volume XV, Number 1, Fall, 1994: "Emma's Crochet"; Fall, 1999, Volume XX, Number 1: "Now"; Fall/Winter, 2005, Volume XXV, Number 1 and 2: "Benches"

The Christian Science Monitor, March 31, 1982: "Starched White Shirts"

The Reach of Song, Georgia Poetry Society Yearbook, 1993-1994: "Rena"; 1994-1995: "Show and Tell"; 1998-1999: "Splintered Moon"; 1999-2000: "Apprentice to the First Born"

The Waugh Street Journal, Volume IV, March 31: "Mrs. Barlow"; "Dogwood"

The Old Red Kimono, Volume XXIII: "Ryan White"; Volume XXIV, Spring 1995: "My Beloveds, I Have Written Your Names"; Volume XXVI, Spring 1997: "The Cowboy"

A Celebration of Southern Poets 50 and Older, Legacies Publications, Brumby Holdings, Inc., 2002: "Playhouse"; "Mother, I'm Afraid"

From GEORGIA POETRY SOCIETY:

CHAPBOOK, *A Species of Ruin*, 1994: "Mrs. Barlow"; "The Bathers"; "Taxonomy"; "The Treecutter's Helper"; "Emma's Crochet"; "Talking Across"; "R. H."; "From Jamie's Window"

CHAPBOOK, *At The Edge*, 2003: "At The Edge"; "Transplanting With Mitsuko"; "Horses in Snow"; "Collisions"; "Withdrawal" (renamed "Inchoate"); "So Very"; "Gone Dancing"; "Whatever of a Holy Spirit"; "Journey"

Acknowledgements

I am forever grateful to the editors of the various journals and magazines who encouraged me with their kindness and patience. I would be terribly remiss if I did not recall the first, the late Collie Owens, Poetry Editor, and Editors Lawrence Hetrick and Marc Fitten, who succeeded him at *The Chattahoochee Review*. Managing Editor Jo Ann Yeager Adkins did more than edit; she became a friend and great encourager. My thanks also go to Dr. Christine Cozzens, whose judgments on my chapbook *At The Edge*, still lift my spirits.

And who would be without the friends who last over the years, forming a circle that allows others in, but never desert their holding places? Such are the *Whimmers* in Rome, Georgia: Bambi Berry, Nancy Griffin, Susan Harvey, and Rena Patton now of Richmond Hill. Each served as examples as they pursued their own arts, but while doing so found time to keep me afloat.

When circumstances removed me from their midwifery, Dr. Janice T. Moore and poets in the North Carolina Writers' Network West created a map of sorts that allowed me for two years to come under their providential influence. Of late, Tom Hutto of Sautee, Georgia, and Annell and John McGee of Cleveland became my staunch support.

For patient, careful editing and constant enthusiasm, I am forever indebted to Dr. Carmen Alcevedo Butcher of Shorter College.

To Carl Griffin, in all capacities: colleague; friend; mentor, teacher to our children; a door-opener and believer for me, my continuing affectionate thanks.

Linda Hill Jordan contributed the gift of time for me to gather my manuscript together. A faithful reader to my husband, she made Thursday mornings islands of R and R during which discordant interruptions of everyday life were abandoned.

Thanks always to Gay Pettit Dellinger, who never stopped listening, and to Sally Edwards, who joined her and created the art for my book/song *Lullaby for Mary*.

Finally, without graphic designer and friend Kelly Byron, and Bill Boling, publisher of Fall Line Arts Press, this book would never have happened. All of you who gave your friendship, take ownership of what you will. I am in your debt.

MWG

Inscriptions

Many of the poems here had their beginning in a relationship with friends, family members, and events connected with them.

I inscribe them here, with thanks for their inspiration.

Emma's Crochet and *Emma's Lullaby*, Emma Lance Reece, in memoriam

Rena and *For a Friend, Thinking of Moving*, Rena Patton

Statistics 101, Mike Burton

For Ari, Ari Turner

Benches and *Christmas Tree*, William Boling

On The Way To Port Matilda, I and II, Philip Greear

Modified, Bambi Berry

Pot Holders and *Safari*, Missy Greear, in memoriam

For Dixie, Dixie Mae Dillon

From Jamie's Window, Jamie Mackay

At Blue Ridge, Nancy Griffin

Surveying Trillium, Teressa Holtzclaw

Weighing, Camping With Delbert, Delbert Greear

Betrothal Gift, Skip and Connie Saunders

Watershed, Myra and Glenn Haynes

Da Capo, Susie Sherrill

Jonquils, Nancy R. Greear

In Storage, Days of Our Lives and *At Susan's*, Susan Harvey

A Cowboy Teaches Creative Writing, Jonathan Hershey

New Baby, Angelina Mia Lazetic-Greear

Explaining to Leah Simone, Leah Simone Holtzclaw

Cary at the Piano, Cary Ruth Greear Ritzler

Transplanting with Mitsuko, Margaret Fields Greear Oren

Let's, India and Tom Lumsden

Global Warming, Bill Holtzclaw

Moving
Gone Dancing

Mildred White Greear

Published by
Fall Line Arts Press
Atlanta, Georgia

ISBN: 978-0-9799379-0-3
Printed in the United States of America

Design by Kelly Byron

Photograph of Mildred Greear by C.B. Backus

Dedicated to

Philip French-Carson Greear

and our children

Carol Greear Carstarphen Backus
Delbert Philip Thomas Greear
Virginia Katherine "Missy" Greear
Margaret Fields Greear Oren
Teressa Templeton Greear Holtzclaw

and to my brother

Alva Thomas White, Sr.

Contents

VII Ars Poetica

VIII. Home Free

Failing to fetch me at first keep encouraged,
Missing me one place search another,
I stop somewhere waiting for you.

From *Song of Myself*
Walt Whitman

I. From Here

At 301 Thirteenth Avenue

Wounded things found their way to my mother's kitchen
where tall windows east and west focused light
into a room already cheered
by a six-eyed, wood-burning cook stove.

Into its cavernous oven went daily biscuits,
weekly tea-cakes, and occasional angel-foods
my mother baked for those who could afford her light touch
and the thirteen egg whites she had them supply.

At those times smell of almond flavoring
tantalized to ecstasy.
If I tiptoed, so that angels wouldn't fall (from Heaven, Yes!) I was allowed
to scrape with fingers the bubbly meringue smears clinging to bowls and beaters.

As unpredictably as angel-foods the oven
might hold chicken eggs my tender brother rescued
from behind a hatchery.
"They are alive! They just need a little more time,"
he would plead, opening his shirt to show
the pippers he was incubating.

Then the oven would be cooled, its door weighted open
and struggling chicks given twenty-four hours' amnesty.

Sometimes it was sightless, almost drowned kittens,
fluffed and put in shoe boxes, prayed over
against pneumonia, that we slid carefully on the bottom rack.

Mornings following such momentous affairs we had breakfast
with cold biscuits from a bin kept for railroad hoboes.
My father would mutter, "I do declare they have marked this house."

I think they smelled possibilities in our chimney smoke
and so brought us their dreams of getting north or south
to jobs or back home, cracked but alive, needing somewhere
to warm over hope, to rehearse stories.
Steam of coffee made especially for them wet words
as they came across the cup,
caused clearings of long silent throats.

Then the oven door was held down by cold hobo shoes,
and smell of travel from last towns erased almond,
tea-cakes, biddies and kittens.

I think the hoboes were most like the kittens,
in need of touch, even if the connection only a saucer.
This received, confidence put them on their roads again.

In lieu of spoken benedictions, in winter my mother
offered squares of flannel, saturated with Vick's Salve
for their promised use in case of colds and coughs.

At their departure the firebox got vigorous shakings;
wood was crowded in until the stove pulsed at maximum.
In just moments water would boil for family tea.

While our father declared, Mother got out cups,
bandaged grievous new knowledge
with no more than the light touch
with which she guaranteed angel-foods
as she passed my chair.

Birds

Before we burned them for family fire
my father drew birds on the smooth boards
from Gilchrist-Fordney Planer Mill where we went
with the wagon built for the goat we found
one day while gathering mayhaws
in far swampy edges of Cotton Mill Pasture.

When we moved from the house of that history
the wagon transplanted more easily than goat
who did not like tethering at all;
certainly not in a yard bounded by railroad tracks.
Action his only language, he informed us by leaving.
Children had little choice.

Wagons wouldn't know the difference, roll
by whatever motive power and going for wood
was a glorious five block adventure...
Down alley to street where a right turn
would take us to another, to cross the very tracks
that in front of our house ran through a cut
so deep we saw only decapitated tops of freight cars
unless we went to the very edge...
Such daring unnecessarily warned against:
Far more to be feared than punishment
were evil spirits goading "Jump!"

Down by the mill the crossing was flat.
Still, ears were nervous for however faint locomotive sounds
coming willy-nilly to deliver logs.
We would charge madly, lifting as much as pulling wagon
across ballast; uncontrollably surrendering to shudders
at once acknowledging and cleansing
from railroad crossing horrors.

Thus expiated we rolled into spaces
mountainous with rejected slabs, redolent of yellow energy.

For free we piled promissory boards
into wagon, and pushed-pulled it home
where my father drew birds.

Was it soft pine sheen that cried *"Birds"*?
Did knots say *Nests* or *Eyes*? Did he read *Birds*
in the crippled look which I knew from tension
in my just-under-the-skin-flesh was sitting stiffly
on my face, had been sitting there as if cardboard
between my skin and me, between my father and me
from the day he refused to play his fiddle for us,
had put his fiddle away forever?

Questions I didn't know how to ask...
But what I saw was his pencil, pocket-knife
sharpened to delicious thin velvet
swoop
powerfully sure;
design once begun, a swift blur
in number two lead as wings grew,
swept back, forward, swerving,
beating, sailing.

Perfect feet perched harmonic
to wings, as if they knew, as if each part
had known from the beginning,
had told the pencil had told the hand
had told my father's eye
how to feather the pulsing under throat,
to join beak open in song, and motion landed
where it had taken flight,
as precise as death, or life.

One bird given me, another begun,
transfixed I watched them multiply;
held them flocking wing to wing, in lucky
circumstances matching tongue to groove
in tight rectangular aviaries
as long as there was room,
then sorted into stacks an order for burning.

Only when coals threatened ash
would we open the heater to make
bird and fuel our differential sacrifice.

Through streaky gaps around the warped top
and holes where nuts and bolts had burned

and rusted away, letting go the manufacturer's
name-plate, I watched as boiling pitch stained
feathers, curled wings upward from charred edges
and exploded like my ten-years-old grief.

But mornings, going down the alley
to join school companions whose houses
uncompromisingly faced proper avenues,
from chimneys planted neatly mid-center
white bungalows neatly mid-center
lawns of winter-grass no goat had,
nor ever would trespass, smoke
smelling of extravagantly purchased coal
burning in numerous grates and furnaces
made me look backward to my father's house.

There, sun caught morning stirred ashes
above skewed chimney, aureoled
in feathered light my father's birds,
sealed his covenant gift.

His art expendable, but his child
was guaranteed the Phoenix,
was prepared for Stravinsky.

Mrs. Barlow

lay on the floor because
it was cooler than on the bed
where sun hit all day. There were
no screens or curtains and scarves
of yellow fire kept winding
from reels somewhere beyond the windows.
Over these as on a floating stage
dust motes danced a halo dividing the world
horizontally. Beneath such cosmic disconcern
my mother bathed Mrs. Barlow's remnant face—
forehead and chin—most of the rest
eaten away by cancer, the first I ever heard named.

"Mrs. Barlow's got face cancer;
she's gonna die," whispered along
sidewalks, the message tying house to house
like the parasitic "Love Vine" linking privet hedges
through and across fences.

When pain let her be hungry
Mrs. Barlow turned her mouth
toward a bowl and Mother spooned
broth sidewise, her face a study of prayer.

Sometimes she sent me to the corner
mattress factory for cast-off ticking
to put on the floor—
something clean for Mrs. Barlow to lie on
which could be burned.

When flies laid eggs in her suppurating flesh
and maggots hatched, Mrs. Barlow was past judging events.
In agony all his own the doctor
said it had occurred to him
they might eat away the corruption,
and he was considering leaving them there.

Something else considered and Mrs. Barlow died;
my mother's tears her last bathing.

Still when I need to measure pain I think
of Mrs. Barlow; want to resurrect her,
for just one conversation make her face whole.

Never having seen it so,
I lend her my mother's.

Fiddler's Child

I remember my father fiddling
on narrow porches
in Cotton Mill Village,
where straight-backed chairs
said one should not expect
too much comfort in this world.

Some adults took the lesson further,
refused to lean against the slats,
held their own backs straight, thank you.
We children sat on the ground.

They never got near a dance tune,
those sober men; never let the music
be in charge; make them forget dancing
was a sin and the line between good
and evil narrower than a bow hair,
that the devil was waiting at every measure
to slide in sidewise between unguarded notes.
That's why they slowed the music down
so slow, filling every empty space,
holding their good ears up, listening to keep that devil out.

One day something must have happened;
maybe a string broke; a lapse announced possibilities;
syncopation threatened; a gap demanded, screamed,
"Move!"

Because by time we children turned eighteen
we everyone had learned to do the Charleston,
next the Big Apple, and then...
then, oh how deliciously wicked,
The Tango.

Playhouse

Where pasture and garden fence corners
met, my earliest playmate and I
wove tall sheathes of bitter weeds
in and out, making green carpet walls
for our vacation house.

Bits of dusty, broken brick
suggested other walls,
their sharp edges pressed easily
into black soil made receptive
from harvesting of spring vegetables.

Carefully observed doorways
got whole bricks, begged
from a father's shop.

Our mothers' kitchens
lent us food; we had lunch,
invited mythical friends to tea,
and dreamed our futures all summer long.

Toward fall, like renters
knowing they would lose their lease,
we became careless,
neglected weekly renewal of our tapestries,
abandoned our freehold to autumn ruin.

Rain raveled weavings
until only pithy stalks
outlined our sagging looms.

Memories, like these, also sag,
but shredded remnants pull threads
through complicated neurons,
precise in their order
as childhood's seasons,
summers soft and green
and bitter weed taste
and smell
a fair fee.

Dancer

My mother was sober; her joys were controlled.
Something had taught her to hide much of her soul;
only those she locked with her
knew the part that stayed free.

I saw her as dancer, nimble in raindrops,
dancing to music
my father's fiddle could never play.
So delicately dancing
until the sweet dream stopped one day.

My mother's first daughter leapt among stars,
my mother's three sons strode a strong wind,
larger than life, their deeds heroic to see;
far beyond me, their worshipful critic,
recorder of their special graces.

Watching them all with such exquisite awe,
I might have been crippled by wonders I saw,
but my loving mother wisely left me her door,
behind which my words and I
practice our hesitant dance.

Starched White Shirts

brought form and smell of wind
into the house, snatched
as they had been from billowing
clotheslines as the storm began.

A light sprinkle from my mother's hand
tamed them to proper size and shape.

Torrents outside could rage,
but where her calm centered
rebellion deflated—the merest
whisper of steam playing a game

of cool-wet
warm-dry

back and forth
back and forth

smoothed shirts and children
as she ironed.

Extracurricula

For months,
my former classmate
wrote columns of nostalgic town history,
building for the climactic event—
a once-in-a-lifetime reunion
of every student who had ever attended
our high school.

Though he wrote well, and authentically
of many events, he never once mentioned
our poverty.

Gave no hint that down in *South City*,
in the *Quarters*
there ever co-existed another high school.

Poor us…we never got to know
never got to hear
Leontyne Price
down there
singing.

Of those so close beside me, which are you?
God bless the Ground! I shall walk softly there,
And learn by going where I have to go.

From *The Waking,*
Theodore Roethke

II. Along The Way

Cora Allison

unschooled, knew more about adjectives
than the sophisticated college educated
family she did laundry for.

Mountain woman…strong muscles
in forearms beautiful through suds
draining from elbow deep washwater,
pulling out sheets to wring, said of another
she'd *never wash a thing for again*:

"She ain't exactly mean.
She just ain't interested."

Interesting, the school teacher mind clicked,
barely refrained from saying out loud.

Later, meeting offending client, Miss Grammar
understood. Cora Allison spoke
a deeper language,
behavioral grammar encoded from knowledge
of human nature, hard won.

The sinner was not *interested.* Would not entertain
a thought from anyone so low on social scale
as to do laundry over a boiling wash pot
in another woman's backyard.

Hypocrisy comes hard with true mountain folk.
As all must, the social leader and Cora Allison died.
I was away, was only told that few paid respects to the former,
and the church had extra chairs brought in for Cora.

Emma's Crochet

Some explanation would have been given
making the extravagance plausible.
Perhaps the hogs had brought more than expected,
or a bushel of the late apples.

But there it was, the gift of thread.
Dear for the sacrifice, for itself,
for the hunger in your hands,
fluttering loom patterns against the coverlet.

It is easy enough for me now, holding the doily,
to trace the wrap-twos, slip-ones;
single, double, and triple-crochets.

Your youngest child gave it to me:
"Mama never had anyone to show her," she said,
"See, none of them are anything alike,
because she didn't have a pattern."

I study it, a deceptively fragile installment
on our wordless connection,
until I understand the vision coming
of how pretty it would be there on the mantelpiece
under the Bible, under the coal-oil lamp,
under that picture of yourself, healthy,
jaunty in a Sunday hat.

I see you making scallops from rain on hedge,
swirling its music into white roundelays,
round and round until the chained song ended,
the birds at last wearied by their darting, darting,
from their perch on your mind's window ledge.

For a Friend, Thinking of Moving

Consider the light you love,
descending from zenith, as tip of cone,
to spread, to bathe all radii
with intensity toward Valley Head,
vertically dangerously;
one should not ride such rays.
Even to look too long might blind.
I have heard that the Vulcan in Birmingham
has been polished to brilliance…wear shades.

And all around in the other directions;
towards Chattanooga, to Lookout Mountain end,
jumping the river, yield to Signal Mountain on the other side;
one need not go so far as that, but watch it wash
over Sand Mountain, pierce deepest gorges
of Big and Little River Canyons;
all, all drowned by the light contained in that cone
whose permanent anchor is *there*
over *that place.*

That place, Mentone,
a spine of its own in the body of your life,
and the inherited house you have inhabited
summer
        after summer,
                                and now
the chance for the acres and the house
where every window you count gives on that light;
no place in any room nor gable surrounds
where light is not affordable.

The light your argument against
whatever practicalities.

Does the realtor not notice
you do not mention *views*,
but only *the light*?

It may be that only you
know the shadows from which you move.

Ryan White

The building you leave is unfamiliar.
(I say it is a newspaper office, my friends argue.)
You throw a heavy looking canvas bag
into your bike basket, kick the stand…
a small dust previews the cloud
at the end of the street.
Cameramen speed to catch you.

They crave a sharp aperitif
for early dinner news. Over your shoulder
you throw one sentence. (My friends and I agree.)
"Leave me alone, I just want to be a normal kid."
Your words bruise like rock; already
from a circumstantial needle, a river of ruin
runs in your blood.

Down the street, papers (I bolster my argument)
hit curbs like muffled shells, presage
the bitter wrinkled message (I have to smooth to see)
the headline
none of us wanted ever to read,
three years later, that you are dead.

Horacio, Por Favor

"I sing because I sing because I sing."
Neruda, *Plenos Poderes*

I am claiming now that "anything"
you kept saying at the airport,
leaving for Santiago de Chile,
only a way of saying thanks, perhaps,
but seriously taken.

What you must do for me now, hombre,
is to go out from Holanda Street,
prepared for hiking a long pilgrimage.
Turn north, then northwestward, going
to Valparaiso, and when there,
out toward a sharp jut of land,
the peninsula of Isla Negra.

Along the way, beg of any peasant
a piece of charcoal from where he fires
his ollas, or cooks his beans.

At Isla Negra, look for the house
of Neruda. It faces the sea, and is surrounded
on three sides by a fence
made of two thousand rough boards,
fifteen hundred of them written upon.

It is for this you need the charcoal.

The boards are dingy from years of greetings:
"Paz, Neruda," some say, others, "Salud,"
and "Sangre de mi hermano."

When you are there, look eastward
toward the mountains he crossed
by mule, fleeing to the Argentine.

Thank them. Pay homage north to heights
of Macchu Picchu where he made covenant
with ancient Incas; then south to soft

vineyard country near Temuco
where he first gave his soul
to nature and his brothers.
Look west again to the ocean,
acknowledge Easter Island
and the far Orient where loneliness
and he drove their hard bargain.

Only after you have done this, amigo,
do the great thing for me.

With the charcoal which will
in the next rain penetrate the earth
write, "Oh brother Neruda,
who sang because you sang
because you sang, I have listened
because I hear because I hear."

Landscape Once Removed

Friend, I now
have been to all those towns
living on your tongue
in far away places.

What a game we played
taking turns
after the Queen's Birthday Ball
at the Australian post—the birthday
Sir Edmund Hillary finished
his Himalaya climb
just in time for.

Lost among one set of strangers
themselves in a set of others
were we drawn
because we shared a continent
for remembering,
alternating loved names of places
we had lived visited married
had children in?
You mentioned Shenandoah—
no one before or since has said
it just that way—the whole valley
took form from your voice—
when I went there
it was exactly as you had called it.

The rivers—the mountains edging
and the towns—always the towns—
the ones you would go back to,
leave again for Africa
and who knows?

Roanoke Radford Big Stone Gap
I have been also to these;
have wanted to stop in some center
and shout your name—

Friend!

"My friend lived here
someone you must have known
she was the one with that odd
nickname the one whose voice
came from under some shadowed pain
in her eyes whose casting sun
I never knew
to float lovingly longingly
over an almost smile
as she recited your names
from her heart's geography."

Lou Vandiver

said I hadn't understood at all,
praising her having hoed all that corn
in the new ground she and Dandy cleared—
you can find it now, on early topo maps
of the Chattahoochee National Forest,
Old Vandiver Fields.

I had imagined her hoe, economical,
shortly swung, scraping ragweed leaves,
silver pale, notched
like young chrysanthemums,
easily told from shiny arrows shooting
from stony clay.

I had imagined her counting strokes
whack, scrape, whack—corn rescued, two-three ears
toward a bushel; had made her my own heroine
when I grew weary of weeding. Told her.

She impatient. "It was the babies, don't you know.
I set'em in holes I dug and lined with linsey-woolsey,
scattered'em where the rows would end, ahead of me,
all through the field."

Her stubby hand reaches, holds my arm;
her eyes, milky with cataracts, see it again,
search mine, testing belief.

"I never thought *corn*, never counted *beans*,
just hoed to my babies. And then
I'd leap-frog'em, start all over again.

And Dandy, when he would come home at night,
don't you know, I'd've hoed the whole field,
and he would say I had done good."

Rena

takes dead birds to the lab,
strips feathers, pins wings,
scalpels back flesh, blows away
with perfectly measured breath
the upward-floating down.

Bends, marks venation,
flexes musculature,
projects bird flying, while
deciding exactly the oak
under which
to bury.

O hawk, O all birds,
so she has handled my poems.

Bared bones, amputated
redundancies, tied
sinew to sinew,
articulating skeleton
stark as truth
for resurrecting flight;
consigning all waste
to burial
in her heart.

Statistics 101

Monotonous as multiplication
the professor's voice droned
reasons for squaring sums
to measure standard deviations.

Below the lecture-room dais,
the interpreter's hands
danced the terms on air;
numbers made arabesques,
pliéd, found, touched,
balanced on new partners;
re-grouped, fluttered
in a pas de deux
trois
quatre
tout le corps!

Momentarily I longed to be deaf
to live so intimately with birds.

The Treecutter's Helper

somewhere between his name
and address
gets lost
can never tell
but one
at a time
take your choice
and put the question right.

His slowness
a gift for seeing
all that space
between
who one is
and where
one lives,

he takes
time
to wander there
knows and imagines
far too much
to tell all at once.

Afghan Woman

Afghan Woman,
tell me your name
so that I can scream you
out of the television picture.

You, you in the blue drape
whose correct name I know slightly;
being generic, less dangerous than yours.

In nightmares one can dream of needing to scream.
In waking hours, I have tried practicing. I always fail.

Why scream when there is neither thief nor murderer
on even the most distant horizon?

But if I had your name, I do believe
I could scream you out of the picture.
Bring you to action, make you fight back;
at the urging of a nation of women's voices
you would run, run, run from the flaying sticks;
from first, second and third persecutor.

Oh woman of no name, Listen! I have picked up your baby
back there. My friends and I are feeding him. We will catch up
and bring him to you. I remember that you were the one in the middle,
against the torn corner of that building
on the right hand of the dusty street
where the men began to flail you.

I will recognize you in the next settlement, or the next
by your flashing eyes, illegally exposed for the gaze of any passer by,
drawn by their intelligence, their direct deep beauty.
Are they the initial stimulus for beating by men whose names we hear?

How is it that I do not know yours and the names of your many sisters?
How is it that we see men's faces, but yours and your sisters' are veiled?
Do your men see themselves so uncomely, unlikely to invite love?

How can I scream you out of the picture; scream to Allah
to make the stick boomerang,

attack the taut nerves of the persecutor, backward,
from hand to shoulder, reverberating the pain to the spinal center
so that flails and clubs fall before they reach you,
crouching, defenseless, unable to run?

Afghan Woman, you of no name, I cry to you. I need to know your name, to know its strangeness change to familiarity. I will listen carefully, repeat lovingly.

Only when I know your name, and you mine, can we proceed
to the next word: SISTER.

My name is Mildred.

For Ari

Ari, if you found them,
you will recognize the two baskets
as what they are: the Easter left-overs.

Just right
for two used birds' nests. One
from the cardinals that
I held you hip-high
to see down into
from the top of the nandina.

The other, the house wren's
with the moss
that hung drooping
out the sides of the candle holder
over the picnic table
we could not use
until six babies were fledged.

These nests will keep well
in the baskets,
and next year
you will decide which to discard
in favor of the other.

I tell you now
baskets are more easily come by
than used birds' nests.

And dear as they all are, nothing
in the scale when measured
against the love between us...So much
that spend extravagantly as we might
the interest will keep us wealthy
and there will always be more left over.

When I moved away
you were nine; I seventy-eight.
Yes, there is enough.

Benches

"Our benches will not sing for us, until our friends have sat upon them."
From the Finnish Epic, *the Kalevala*

Dear Friend, you have sat upon our benches;
the whole house sings, beyond the sadness of your leaving.
So everywhere the music, dancing began; all things
have to be restrained. The dining chair
dances so that wine spills and rolls on plastic cover
so judiciously placed over the cotton sheet
masquerading as linen last night for the banquet
where smallest words like fading fireworks landed
and kept clinging to cups, saucers and the crumb cake.
I shake jewel sentences from the careful napkins.

Meanwhile window panes loosen in their frames; I fear
they may shatter from the light of your left-over gaze.
Should this happen, I shall send you great bills from the glazier.
He will ask how on earth such a thing occurred
and I will have to confess that we had a sorcerer here.

Do not let the account disturb you. It has, as always
been paid in advance, your company being beyond price,
beyond calculation, even though the house may unsettle
from its foundation. The benches being so out of control.

On the Way to Port Matilda

I

"On a Sunday in October
in 1930 I came up here."
He is sure of the date
because both brothers who brought him
had come home for visits
and the oldest drove the green Dodge.

"We were looking for chestnuts—
can you believe we found them?
Fall was early—took home
an almost bushel
already out of their burrs."

His hands move against each other,
feel the long ago velvet
of the underside hull,
the polished softness it gave
to the inner shell.

This heart of things
he would keep searching for
far beyond the gap at Unicoi,
other mountains;

Gaps giving way to coves
between synclines, anticlines,
where he would read rocks
and ages of rivers that cut them,

To take away, share,
once he peeled back bristling spines
kernel truths of wheres
and whys,
bring home at least
an almost bushel—enough to satisfy
me and the children.

II

"Bald Mountain," he says.
"There stands Bald Mountain," he says.
Then, "Enotah Bald Mountain," he says.
As if repeating the name
makes sure of it.

This is one way he worships,
sees himself in God's image
now, naming the creations.

He nearly always begins
with mountains.

Emma's Lullaby

Rune a by, croon a by,
my little one,
Rune a by, croon a by,
my pretty one.
Sweetest little baby boy under the sun.

I've tethered you a cloud
to the hemlock tree;
it's promised to shade you
when need might be.

Stones said they will play you
a rainbow colored tune
and the creek splinter magic lights
under the moon.

Fairies will invite you
to where rabbits play,
innocence always
your right of way.

Rune a by, croon a by, my darling one,
prettiest little baby boy under the sun.

I'm making you a song
for every care you'll ever own.
I asked the wind to sing it
and I threw the wind a bone.

The wind heard and promised
since you lack a toy
to fill skies with prosy birds
for my little boy.

Promised to move gentle
for a while to let you sing,
and smooth away corners
from many a harsh thing.

This is my gifting song;
you are one-day old.
It's bought with the sum
of my heart's gold.

Rune a by, croon a by, my little one,
dearest little baby boy
under the sun.

Augury

He is more Indian than he knows
as he douses evidence of his hopes,
taking it slowly, room by room.

Her subtly living shadows
were first to go, a careful closet
smothers their perfumes, stills dances
and bird flutterings.

He has swept the bureaus clean—
lastly her desk, which, if he were to pray
orthodox prayer, he would use for altar,
pray her back here for a book, a note,
to smile across it with some special absurdity.

His bargain is stricter than that
and his visible house empty of her
as villages devoid of light
before the high priest would climb
the holy mountain to confirm the sun.

Like the priest he knows
the sun must reappear for its own sake,
renewing a cycle unconnected with duty,
with earth beacons; benevolent by choice.

As weeks lengthen he practices, closes
his eyes against imagined incandescence;
grows patient, becomes deaf for a footstep
if already sorrowful for his pain, she chooses
to let the sun reflect her in the moon behind him.

Modified

I

My life proceeds warily between adverbs;
Yes and *No* are threatening meridians
converging on a wobbly pole.

Southeastward and southwestward
stretch their shadow vectors, *Forever,* and *Never.*

I distrust the destination of each:
wish to deny their symbiosis,
turn my compass, nervous
to find some latitude for *Maybe.*

II

It is always the vectors
that deflect us.
One hundred eighty degree paths
that would insure arrival
get bent by circumstances
taut as laser,
sabotaging by a degree here,
quantum leap there.

Adrift, adrift,
we tack in such uncertainties
on waters becalmed or stormy.

The compass holds true; it is we
who no longer relate.
Where were we when we last read true North?

Unrecorded longitudes spin beneath us.
We move;
our arrival perhaps on time;
the destination the big surprise.

May Pole

There is something at the center of things...
An unnamed thing; the smallest of points
around which all the energy of the thing spins,
like the ribbons coming from the top of the May Pole
with which we children once welcomed spring...
turned into something not lovely by a political event
thousands of miles away from the hard packed clay yard
around our school house.
While it was still lovely, the streamers coming undesignated
so far as I knew, until, there in my hand, a carefully cut roll
of pink crepe paper; the color I loved from sweet peas
in my teacher's garden across the street. My task on the count
of one two three go, to follow the lead of the person ahead to my right,
and the colors swirled like music from the calliope. A director
could change designs by sending pinks among blues or greens,
wherever she wanted, and soon the embroideries were multicolored,
and single strands plaited like long hair braids.
Around and around, and gentle drifts of air billowed Sunday school
skirts; sashes like the crepe paper dancing back and forth, making
me feel elegantly special from their soft swishing. I was doing my part
and it was all entirely beautiful.
What happens to that kind of thing: What disconnects us from that center,
so that an event of one person's making can undo
the innocence and beauty of a whole universe?
And at the end of my philosophical journey,
what is left is a still straggling wisp in my memory
of too tightly stretched crepe paper, scattering across
landscapes...the center of the energy still there, somewhere,
somewhere where the planetary system anchors and turns and turns
and turns.
Colors stream out through the galaxies, but I cannot reach
the end of the paper that has my name on it.

A wind sways the pines,
And below
Not a breath of wild air;
Still as the mosses that glow
On the flooring and over the lines
Of the roots here and there.
The pine-tree drops its dead;
They are quiet, as under the sea.
Overhead, overhead
Rushes life in a race,
As the clouds the clouds chase;
And we go,
And we drop like the fruits of the tree,
Even we,
Even so.

From *Dirge In Woods,*
George Meredith

III. In Dark Places

Again This Summer

the middle sisters
have come, have brought their sons,
their daughters, their patterns and plans
for sewing on the back porch.

The children are all of a size,
give or take a few darts or pleats,
and one mother cuts while the other
sews or makes button holes.
The first garments are the better made.
There is time for French seams, lace,
matching eccentric plaids.

Nothing is too complicated
until invitations to tea parties,
imagined and real, tree house building,
and calls from home pull at calendar
selvages. New schedules fray
the days' warp and towards the end
I am more often at the machine.

My daughters' voices hum mutual assurances,
a background steady counterpoint
to the electric needle. Each garment
that is not perfect now will fit
by fall, surely by Christmas.

As I listen I wish that time
wove on the bias; to stretch
like the casing I sew for the drawstring,
to gather up, to ease out, to allow
somehow at the end of the days
a hem for letting down a few more hours.

Pot Holders

one day someone will empty the closet
take down from the shelves
the made-as-on-assembly-line pot holders

the ones she saw
from far away office days like letters
outer envelopes ready for stuffing
the stuffed ones the stuffed and sealed ones

the stuffed and sealed and bundled ones
waiting for unknown zip codes
but all directed toward abeyance of pain
a frantic busy-ness of cutting ripping tearing
old sheets towels shirts jeans
old pot holders themselves to sandwich
between covers created without discrimination
for pattern thread color thickness size

rather like slash/burn
in a cloth forest grown through years of sewing
big pieces make small small pieces make big
grab cut rev machine turn stack
make stuffings don't look
stuffstuffstuff
stack

after supper whipwhipwhip
the open edges stackstackstack
count compulsively
every ten to shelf

No one ever had too many pot holders
she reasons when she reaches one hundred
assesses her own mortality wonders
will the person who finds them
be wise enough to ask

What manner of grief was this
made into cushions
against fire?

Safari

The dress you wore in the picture…
The one Our Lady of Perpetual Help School
used in the yearbook memorial….

Ah yes, that dress…how we laughed
that it should fit each of us,
you voluptuous, I bean pole.
I say it did have style!
Long waist, the wonderful hip-slung belt
I had made at Bob's Shoe Store…
beautiful leather and bold brassy buckle;
it was the wrongly sized belt that made
the creation affordable in the first place.
Precision top stitching on epaulets,
all those pockets, and in perfect khaki!
What else to call it but our Safari Dress?

Uncanny that two years after you retired it,
you resurrected it for school pictures.
Dressed it up with a scarf, complimented
it further with the simple chain.
Adorned it, us, your students, our world
with your straightforward gaze.

And the smile…we know
you were about to laugh out loud
but something in your eyes
says you thought better of it, and so
it is only promissory….

We are to keep waiting for that,
for it to reach us from the far back edge
of the light years
where you wander
on your special, most distant of all safari.

For Dixie

Fair granddaughter, yes, you
of the copper braids,
indeterminate blue eyes,
whose prism I have held to light before
but, as now, not captured—
it's you granddaughter
who does this water dance with me—
each near drowning in calamitous grief—
our gasping not synchronized
makes bubbles from meager oxygen—
the tight film implosive.

I feel the danger of too close approach,
knowing your distaste
for uninvited touch, yet believing together
we could successfully tread the pain.

But for now accept that I do not know
how our ballet will end,
only cry that if one day your pas seul
has you smothering, come up, come up,
push with all energies
to embrace the horizon, reach
for your grandmother's persistent love
there to cushion you if you will allow.

Something Underground

Something underground knows,
directs Queen Anne's Lace
to carrot beds; morning glories
to all domestic beans.

Nightshade appears on cue
in potato and tomato rows,
leaf offered in kinship to one,
blossom to the other.

Wild onions everywhere destroyed in lawns
prosper from care farmers lavish
where they blend with Bermudas, Vidalias.

I try to accommodate,
do not begrudge the space,
hope wild ox-eyes
when they come to Shastas
will observe a respectful truce.
I will water them all,
mindful of other plantings,
stranger migrations through soils
whose particulars I do not yet know.

Perhaps that Something Underground
will sort my cells correctly,
send them tunneling to germinate
in safety where you are, for a while
to be with whatever that beauty
you have by then become.

All Songs That Have Been Mine

All songs that have been mine for singing have been sung.
Nor knew I then for whom the singing was, nor if the songs
should happy be or sad. It has been so as when a bell is rung
and each succeeding wind to bear it so prolongs

each note one loses sense of individual tone
that first had sounded. All it was or grew to be
on weighted air survived by chance alone
incorporate in changeling monody

that had no mood save for the listening ear.
If I should sing them now, they would be sad.
You are not here to hear.

And Her Increase Forever

At six, Tempy, you could not have dreamed
of knowing a man; but what matter?
The two men, buyer and seller had you,
owned you the way they owned a cord of wood,
a harness, but the way they owned you
was not what they owned you for.

You were female to be bred.
If you were to sicken, or die within two months of sale
from brother to brother
it was to be the seller's loss, not to mention yours.

No loss of money;
the two hundred and fifty dollars
you brought would be repaid.

What power to hurt lies now,
one hundred and sixty two years later
in the faded writing that conveyed not only you,
but your "increase forever to him and his heirs forever."

When you became a woman, Tempy
and wanted to give yourself and your husband
a child, did that knowledge keep you barren?
A record found once in Pennsylvania
says you married at age thirteen.

I have a friend that age; she has worn braces
on her teeth to make them even more beautiful.
She plays a game called soccer, running, and kicking
large balls; she makes music on something like the pianoforte
reported to have been in your owner's house.

Most of all she laughs and imagines many things.
She dreams of growing up and having children.
What did you imagine, Tempy?
What did you dream for your increase forever?

At the Cemetery
(Peek-a-boo)

My daughter,
the one who knows such odd phenomena
tells me this thing.

In every culture of the world, there is a game
equivalent to *Peek-a-boo.*

It derives, she says, from urgent need
for object fixation.

The tiniest, newest of the newborn
will find its mother's face. Will cry
for it if it disappears for long.

Loving mothers reassure. Play a game
of disappear, reappear. Bird hands
fly over to cover, then fly away.
Mother, Daddy, significant other comes back.
They always come back.
They will always come back.

Time Passes

One grows bored with bird hands,
the opening and shutting eyes.
New games for old.
Teddy Bears hide under blanket
and bed. They are found.
Laughter, relief.
Oh purest relief.

Time Passes

Hide-and-seek under the corner street light
used for home base. Hider and seeker comfortable
changing roles. The light is always there.
One will find one's way home, from dark, to light.
Peek-a-boo is alive and well.

Until

Beloveds leave beloveds to sleep
in cemeteries others built for them.

They become ancestors by nothing they do,
but by what we do...our simple act of living
a generation or two beyond them.

They cannot reassure us; we reassure ourselves,
seek their small real estate, make pilgrimage
to unfamiliar cities,
follow maps to mounds and depressions,
decipher names
on pitted marble, granite; rub tracings
across splintered wooden crosses,
desperate for that face
closed, hidden by tombstone,
the tombstone, the hands
over the eyes
that we cannot pull away.

Anno Domini

Some were dined
and some were wed
and there were those
who cursed their bread.

Some sought water,
some sipped wine,
some found nectar
pickle brine.

And those who sang
with those who danced
by their rightness
so entranced

Had no dirge
of grief to spare
for children breathing
death from air.

Casualty

Flags furl on the street past my window
and drum beats invade through the door.
The tramping march
of many feet
pounds over my heart's floor.

It's always the older who plant the war,
and lives of the young they are reaping.
So listen, dear daughter,
and listen, dear son,
this is your mother speaking.

The commanders, the colonels, the captains
use words patriotic, ideal....
The cities laid waste?
Dead enemies? Great!
And it isn't our business to feel.

The pictures they show at the end of the day
are always of death, but of others.
Dear daughter, dear son,
from the drums turn away,
it's not soldiers you're killing, it's mothers.

Amputated, they know, at the message,
all hope of their healing receding;
they grope here and there
to name limbs that are gone
are perplexed not to find where they're bleeding.

Habeas Corpus

Beat the drum
who sired the son
and sent him forth to kill.

Let her mourn
whose son was born
to do another's will.

But scorn the age
whose sordid sage
could spawn such rotting ill.

Taps

I write to the drums past the window.
I write to the drums past the door.
I write to the beat of a tall lad marching.
(What sons can the big drums restore?)

Marching. Marching.
The drums are beating away, away,
and my heart beats too,
but the drums beat out
more fears than my heart can say.
(Why marching the tall lads today?)

Big drums are not for skipping along.
Tall lads do not skip I know.
But a toy drum beats out funny little booms
for any way feet might go.
(I know, for I've heard them before.)

But now for the beat of the big big drums
and the sound of the feet past the door
where the drums beat loud
but not too loud
to silence the heart in the door.

(What sons can the bugles restore?)

M.B.,

My brothers brought their uniforms
home from wars. In season
we wore the khaki pants and shirts
to blackberry patches,
could trust that good chino to turn
a briar away; tied a string around
leg bottoms sprinkled with sulfur
to keep chiggers out.

Later, buttons and zippers stored
in baskets stuffed with matriarchal salvage,
remnants swaddled new puppies and kittens,
once a lamb. Whatever remained
from tender ministries washed cars.

But you didn't take your things.
I bought your shirt, clean,
in perfect condition, your name
still bold on collar facing,
at the army-navy store.

Wore it with blue polka-dot pants
to the riverboat party;
mood lightheartedly chic
until the river went eerie
at a too-sudden dusk.
The boat splintered
a thousand wavering moons.
Engines strained against throttling down;
conflicting energies muted voices,
faded syllables to language
I no longer understood. Foreign deltas
formed from familiar creeks;
foliage turned tropical.
This was patrol.

It was for me the boat was slowing.
My assignment clear. I was to follow you,
scouting the mist all the way,

the white strands luring.
So strong this experience
in new cities now
I search for you, names like yours
in directories,
forestalling the inevitable,
the day I wear your shirt,
go read the black marble wall.

Going into Mississippi Dark

Going into Mississippi dark,
keeping speedometer steady as time
flowing out of Georgia's five A.M. rain...
not thinking miles...
just wanting fifteen degrees of geography
succeeding into middle Alabama
ahead of sun
realizing darkness kept around me
funnels me into that other darkness
felt remembering Mississippi childhood.

It's only the delta land that's black
but something not soil colors the atmosphere
southward, eastward, wherever,
eats like acid and leaches dark upward
weighting already heavy air.

Memories bubble from magma,
pull me into that psychic space,
physically my birth room
where I was not supposed to be at night.

Someone had put me there
before the waves of white figures
had finished passing down our block.
For a while they must have forgotten.

Fear as instinctive as breath
surely would never be again as great, but was,
seeing one white shroud enter my mother's room
and dissolve into my father...alive...not white...
not ghost, but grotesquely normal,
calling my name, opening his arms to me,
which I would never freely enter again...
doomed at five to be his dark judge.

My mother took me to a space
I should have known well, but cannot remember.

The exact scenario never repeated,
relived in staccato instances...
photographs of klansmen in parades...
contests for the best essay on KKK history
with big cash prizes from the UDC...
an uncle's taboo offer of secret klan greetings
for my entry. I can repeat it still,
but never wrote the paper.

Grief and shame united
when I learned the word *lynching*,
heard *nigger*, saw remnant crosses
through our small town.

Most painful to figure out why a woman,
shy as I, who had begun to smile at me
from behind her side yard hedges
as I passed going to school
one morning sat hunched and moaning
on her back steps, looking at me
with a message I could never decipher.

A purple blue distributed over her swollen features.
Through her bruised lips there were broken teeth,
bleeding gums. A partly burned cross in her front yard
frightened me to near paralysis.

I will not call her name, though seventy five years later
I still remember it, as well as the effort it cost
not to ask my mother why it had happened,
and to tell me, if that time, long
long ago...
and if my father had...
and could he still?

Beside me my sister's voice mercifully enters my memories,
begins reciting familiar names.
They shine from river bridges and city limit signs
in the car's determined tunneled light.

Oh Mississippi names!
Beautiful as legend; bitter as Indian tears,
black men's blood.

You are mantras swaddling me for backwards birth
into that womb where fears of knowing
crowd and crowd.

It is too much for me. I slow the car,
stop for coffee. Back on the road, I linger
until light from Georgia touches me,
palely illumines the road ahead.
Then accelerate in proportion
to my sister's growing excitement.

I am going home at all costs.
I have promised.

R.H.

In the south Mississippi jail
where four years of thirty
have ticked from his clock
my friend decorates envelopes
with scenes of rivered forests.

Not allowed pens or brushes,
what needs outlining he draws
in pencil. A few magic markers
make his palette.

Once I watched him paint iron tables
and chairs on my patio,
his touch carelessly certain
on the flat interstices,
the rounded trailing curlicues.

As I paint these now the oily black
rolls off and through the stamped grills,
spattering drop cloth and far beyond.

I hurt remembering his patience
as if he had all the time in the world
to make rigid ivy leaves
smooth to the touch as flowing water.

His envelope river does not flow smoothly;
currents slash so forcefully
one fears the paper will wash apart,
spill, drown words in cataracts.

Only the laurel can hold it,
rooted from the water's edge upward
and upward to hemlock and rimless sky.
His destiny days bordered by pumice
and worn steel, my friend is not yet stingy
with his dreams; always the laurel
is in full bloom, pink, so pink.

Tectonics

At Riverside, California, Rubidoux Mountain
jags against the sky, its peaks
systolic, magnified upward thrusts
of the machine over the bed we turn away from
to look out windows of ICU.

We are all floating on magma,
uncertain footing in the best of times,
now shaking our private lives
with out-of-sync aftershocks.

My husband floats most delicately
of all, as electric waves bear him
up and down, up and down. He helps himself
only by not hindering; surrenders
to pulses mathematically relentless
as crustal plate aggression, withdrawal.

The mountains are all that move
more slowly than my breath, unconsciously paced
to match the green graph, and I go up and down,
up and down, following Rubidoux, San Gorgonio
as they cut the sky in two, their terminals
overlapping lesser-knowns except at the one spot
where a gap forms, and my eyes
leap across,
refuse to acknowledge the break
where systole and diastole
millennia ago eroded
from mountains, to deserts
and horizons toward forever.

Horoscope: March 1-31
To a Certain Libra

The garden party is already ruined;
your watered silk dress in tatters
crucified against rose hedges escaped to
from falling canopies. Briefly
sashes and garden hat ribbons will color
the lightning.

The orchestra will not get past tuning
notes meant to dissuade the storm.
It will be outplayed; something else will drum.
Everything will be loud-pedaled.

Words you planned perfect as prayer
will reverse as static on the fractured air,
join chaos. Tautened to breaking
component syllables will amputate consonants,
eviscerate vowels, implode in galactic burial.

No breath will pulse against space
to echo they were there.

This one Mild-Lamb's day has outdone you.
Do not take it personally. The wind
does not know how you will rue
the shredded afternoon, look one day
for a hat you almost remember,
or that most in the world
of too deep to be spoken sorrows
it will be an aborted message
that you mourn.

By Whatever Degree of Sun

The peach grew far too ripe
before falling,
beyond preserves,
beyond brandy,
only a seed
around which rotting pulp
would wash away in September rain
(if the drought broke)
or corrugate, unrecognizable,
beyond resurrection:
by just that same degree
the first persimmon
chanced falling, so bitter-green
the least experienced forager
would know to avoid it.

I sole witness
to the simultaneous events
accepted burden of interpretation,
declared to self aloud
that for some things
it is far too late
and for others
too early
to hope.

Straight Shift

Listen up, you paupers, you bums,
and your families headed for the potters' field.
Be careful when you die; don't go planning
no Sunday funeral.

No matter what DFACS says of circumstances,
it's one to two-thirty, Monday through Friday.
Later than that, there's the matter of overtime
and already the city has forked over six hundred
and ten bucks to men operating the back hoe
to open and close your six by six by three.

The county has laid out seven hundred and fifty
for a box, and they are not digging any deeper.

Now babies, them pitiful little ole babies are different.
Hours the same, but cost a little less.
They go up there by the regular monument trade
and nobody can look and say
who was free and who wasn't
provided sooner or later there's a stone.

Enough of that. We'll dig you all down fair and square,
even pull our hats off as we tamp you decent.
Might spare you a backward wish, but understand:
no overtime.

Family Friend

I have been given your name,
relic from your grave before granite
was ordered—letters cast as linotype
on sprayed bronze-copperish background—
the alphabet and dates of your too-short life—
a bottom line unit-cast,
advertising the funeral home—above these
a laurel wreath, standard design
accompanying the no frills burial.

Like the logo, this does not move
under my tracing fingers as do the letters
of your name. With the slightest of tools,
a hairpin, fingernail file, even a toothpick,
I could free them from their encasement,
perhaps then consign what is left
to recycling at Anderson's Scrap Metal
where a pound of almost anything
brings but a penny.

What shall I do? Your daughter's companion
forced it upon me. "Wait, wait. You must take it.
Every afternoon she would get it
out of the car here on the back seat
where she kept it; hold it with her arms folded over.
Takin' my mama for a walk,
she'd say, and no one to stop her but me
and I quit trying."

Now her granite side by side with yours
and I sole possessor of a transient name
almost become your photograph, and yes,
portrait too of your self styled
Wild Sagittarius Child, elusive, vague
to incomprehensible, your name moving,

your life moving ever so slightly
against its rigid frame.

I do not know what to do
with your name,
other than taking it with me
to my wherever homes.

Accessory

Marshmallows
stick memories together
ambiguous feelings of being seven
years old, and hungry,
but old enough to know
it was not to be talked about.

You, oldest of us, at fifteen
allowed to work at Woolworth's
though it was illegal, bringing home
your dollar fifty for a ten hour day
and giving it to Mother
as you always did…had to
being conscience driven…
but where
did the marshmallows come from?

Not from your pay;
we younger ones knew
not just from having seen
you give it all to Mother,
but from the way
you brought them to our beds that night.
A huge package. I remember
the way they pushed against the cellophane,
stuck together when I tried to hush them
as I pulled out what I hoped my reasonable share.

How could I, being so sure
you had stolen them,
have eaten them
so greedily?

Inchoate

In the beginning there must have been
words to say. They are gone. As lost
as the froth of echoes; word ghosts,
whose if-ever meanings turn gibberish.
Gone as foam on a dying wave, whose last
energy implodes its image from the air.

My realities turn inward:
inchoate syllables battle only
for breath to speak your name.
          Your name.
                    To speak your name.

Words

I. Con Brio

Next time, I will speak words.
I will say words,
crystalline,
glissanding
as waterfalls.
And I will be
in the beginning.

II. Diminuendo

My pretty words were all I had for you.
A rosary recitatif of fervent quietude.
Syllables polished as stones from the sea
where nymphs called you
to see them dance
to guitar music
louder than
my rosary.

The nymphs and guitar
outspoke my words
and now, I hold broken syllables
look for distant hyphens
to make an ellipsis connection
so I can say, "Oh, will someone take my words
only slightly used—
left over just today
unclaimed at my salvage office.
My pretty words
    My words
        My prett..."

Remainder

We are not remembering things alike.
While facts, your specialty, tend to convince
one of their importance, I no longer care
to know what time it was, on what date,
exactly what was said, or what that funny name was.

What I need you to remember with, not for me,
is the way the leaves
fell over the path to the tea house,
the sounds of the bamboo whisk
barely touching the ceremonial cups;
the shock of that too-sweet cake
with the bitter tea.

Afterwards, the walk along the inland sea
where molecules surging tightly against one
another, and me, were my bodily connection
with home, if I liked, or from which I could
disconnect, which I did, climbing terraces
to where you stood under satsuma trees
offering miniature suns to the Oishima sky.

Wanting you to remember this,
and numerous other kinds
of many marriages, I grieve
that I cannot be in your memory
to extract the difference
between exactly what it is that you forgot
or never knew.

Cataclysm

Positive of electric danger of mutual touch, our hands
instead sieved rocks, our wordless grief
against reflected moon, made thousands
of crepuscular splinters, multiplied
fractiles above and below the falls.

Turbulence replicated
        delivered
                drowned
them in oceans
still radiating energy
        to drive metabasalt
                to spread
                        to move continents
such was the power
of what was surrendered there.
So my heart believes.

Sostenuto

While other lovers
swam, surfaced, caught breath
in lyrical oceans, tidal harmonies
effortless as Middle C,

Like amputees denied
the full scale, the inversions,
we returned to safe shores
from where we only listened

And heard out perfect inventions
invented again. Cacophonies
hurling rebellious colors
against too thinly strung skies

Orchestrated our failures fortissimo
stopped rehearsals just short
of resolution,

Left us sustaining
on the sonorities
of the diminished seventh.

To My Sister

I want your spirit rebellious like the starling's
as it makes its territorial quarrel heavy, important,
sending it abroad in garden, and into this room
where I watch by your bed, my heart congestion
anguish at how the road curves too soon,
how time speeds and how small the space
to bury grief.

I want your voice not raspy, smothery from fluids,
but pure on air as when we were excitable children,
you calling: *Listen to the shell; ocean waves are dancing.*

I want your eyes to look at me, not search
beyond for something we have mislaid or lost.

Most assuredly I want your ankles not swollen
black with blood. I want them flesh pink and thin
as they arc up, then down into a perfect dive,
you urging me as you weave the water:

Come on, jump in, you ninny—it's not too cold
And I am not going to let you drown.

Too Soon

I was looking at the clock when the cloud
enveloped me. It was ten A.M. on a day
not meant for clouds: meant for songs I had sung
because you were coming; meant for blue air
if we should measure sky; for mosses crushed
to cushions if we should walk in woods.

If life were kind, you would stay to watch cool
mountains curve against a wavering moon. Instead
a sharp stricture cut breath. Something desperate
sped pendulums, threw time forever awry.
From that moment to reference important events
I would say "before"

and "after." When the telephone voice confirmed
my dark spy's message I did not flinch with word
that you were dead; begged only of whatever gods
to never know like that again.

They have been merciful.

In the Waiting Room

Question mark backs
bend and bend and bend
from that one day
when shoulders first sagged
barely one cell stronger
than will to straighten,
and the next time
and the next, and one day
the suit coat slipped downward
from the arm line
and one day the suit coat
hiked up in the back
and made unsightly points
below the front waist, hanging, it seeemed,
halfway to the knees.

Hands thrust in pockets pretend
it's all on purpose…
the leaning, the pushing…
you were not ready
to apologize yet.

The bones keep cringing,
inexorably get their own momentum;
lungs, liver, heart, pancreas,
all feel pressure, caught in a vise
relentless as starfish
latched on oyster, doomed to explode,
unable to keep body door closed
against that suction.

There is something smothery about this,
and little choice between
explosion and implosion
as tissue yields to bone.

The body foreshortened to little more
than half its height,

eyes stretch sockets to look forward,
will never again read sky...
Only a circle of earth in full and constant view
reminding you. You are getting
in diving position.
Ready to go.

In the Laser Surgeon's Office

No one speaks.
It is as if words
kept in check
from naming fears
between appointments
might hemorrhage,
take vitreous humor
in floods
over the carpet;
under the door clearing,
rushing to elevator shafts,
drowning emergency exits,
stairwells,
in salty ropy oceans
too horror filled
for any except
the already blind
to enter.

Spatial Episode

A line of sky
falls away
south of the moon
catches on the ridge
deflects eastward
vibrates firs
tortured branches
of Virginia pines
weaves through hemlock
fronds dipping
under weight of light
so anciently so oppositely
cold.

From high
on the gap it cuts
with this shallow creek
to anchor
on arbutus
its paled to ivory pulse
having returned to the cosmos
whatever of color
was economical
for the exchange.

My math does not extend
to Quarks and their derivatives
cannot measure cost in energy
for angle of refraction
seducing my vision.

Somewhere here however
is a triangle from Moon
arbutus and me.

Ancient formulae dissolve.

Nothing can deal
with such unsteady hypotenuse
tinged pink now
trembling
through treed distances.

The ill malinger in their beds
As pain through all their members spreads
And have not strength to die
And the world so beautiful.

From *At Autumn Things Are All At Odds,*
in THE SEASON OF FLESH,
Byron Herbert Reece

IV. And The World So Beautiful

For the Time Being

I breathe
I am keeping
the world alive
it cannot end
if I keep living

I will do my duty
having loved earth well
having been given good reason

What debts
can be satisfied
when exchanged goods
come in thousands
of birds
against October's
cumulous skies
and scent of shriveling marigolds
freshened
as winds settle low

I obey my instinct
to honor such obligation

No matter how hard it gets
I will
keep breathing
keep time alive
until it must be handed off
entrusted
to those
determined as I

To keep on living
all that is required
just for the time

Being

At the Edge

Was it spring?
There was a certain light,
the windows open,
those strange windows we had
in that house, casements, opening out,
no screens, nor any feeling
that what flew in
would stay for long,
everything free in the easy air.

There must have been birds somewhere
for now, when the memory stirs
it is when doves flurry upward.

I am never prepared for this,
not having seen them come to feed;
only hear at some breakfast sound,
scrape of spoon on bowl, crack of an egg,
the upward flutter, catch glimpses
of grays and browns vague as the memory
of no event.

Just the feel; through the open windows
something critically important
was going to happen
if I waited.

It throbbed on the promising air.
Something wonderful was going to happen
if I waited.

It was on the air
flowing over me in
over me out
through the open windows.

Christmas Tree

Going after the Christmas tree, strangely
opening talk is of earth's entropy. "I judge
my mortality," he says, "with easier equilibrium
when I remember Earth is dying too.... Our sun,
right now, as we. I feel so related when I remember that.
I love Earth more."

We take the sharp turn then that leads directly
to a hollow, where he holds option on the land.

I watch: my reality, and his dream.
A rectangular pond for watering
long-gone cattle becomes a lake, following
gentle contours. There, the watershed drains
lazily to store twenty feet deep water for diving;
acreage expanded for canoes and kayaks.

A slumping barn, straightened, repainted, houses
a horse...maybe two. A section for many hens.
There will be Leghorns and Barred Rocks,
and Rhode Island Reds. Their eggs of subtly
different colors, and oh yes, an Auracana
for that beautiful Easter blue.

His still young daughter will love that; he projects
to grandchildren; leverage against reluctant
wife and older children.

We climb a rise, not so much for tree as glances
of the opposite ridge. He will buy all of that,
and enough beyond, down the backward slope
so no building will push above his horizon.
He will save every bordering pine.

Turning again to the slope we first confronted,
we measure the house by which way the light will fall.
Here will be the broad front porch, and there the large kitchen.
There must be a good chimney for mandatory wood-burning stove.

He goes down imagined steps to grounds covered with jonquils.

A sweep of arm embraces the entire estate; unexpectedly
closes arc at windfall tree...seemingly dead
but sending from desiccated bole a shoot, perfect.

A gentle smile accompanies courtesy paid to age
as he asks me to take turns with the saw,
and back home, for one more year, the tree
is judged prettiest we have ever had.

My eye on the short range...his on the long, I make
an omelet from blue eggs, and plan tree decoration.
He eats, and asks, "How many chicks
should I really begin with? How long before they lay?"

But short or long, projections have moved from entropy:
there is proportionate time for all we plan to do.

Especially will we love Earth more.

Seasons

Now that November has come,
not by the calendar, the numbers
chasing across the year's pages,
but by the brown leaves' declarations
written on the earth,
Behold what was bronzed from green to gold
to crimson and orange laced edges
to cushion the earth are fallen!

No recent remembered rain has wrought this change.
It has taken root from underneath, from early September
when the branches flooded
and rivers crested here, there, everywhere
and the earth could do nothing but drink and spill.

Now dead colors ooze under foot;
shorn of glory, of recalled persimmons,
cardinal flowers and purple ageratums
for November bleached, as alchemist,
dyed, darkened and swallowed them all.

When was first warning?
That first goldenrod,
first queen of the meadow...
was that only in September?
When did that first maple leaf crispen,
curl to something dark in our hand...
surely that was August...August, so wise sounding,
so regal...prophesying?

And what then...if it were August
and November autumn
there in hiding,
dear heart,
let it be so,
if I should look, now, could I find
now that November has come,
April hiding here?

From Jamie's Window

Morning pushes a gasket-thin wedge
across the eastern canyon brow,
hinges against the western edge
pries upward the cupped, lidded dark.

Runnels of light finger routes, filter
to fields a thousand feet below.

For hours the interplay will grow
two of everything:
shadow for tree
tree for shadow.

Toward noon the valley
reduces to integer, for a space
everything so particulate that from my aerie
I could lean to move
a single leaf. Instead,
focus as a doe nudges her fawn.

Together
they climb the light.

Past noon, shadows reverse, pivot east,
paint brown camouflage. Morning's upward
corridors blend to dusk. Dark imperative
as light, the deer descend.

Tomorrow
they will clock the day
again; for a brief season
confirm the sun.

Talking Across

Leaning out upstairs windows
of skinny apartments
the two women could be
deco art, vivid blue, fuchsia
airbrushed on tired
public-housing brick.

Faces glisten black lacquer wet
as conversation ruptures
strictured silhouettes.
Hands travel out with words,
throw weighted meanings.

Bound only by air
the agenda moves as it will
from absurdities to heartbreak
and back again
as I dream their words in living color.

Now sentences swirl
in proper cartoon
balloons, fall in downdraft,
bounce over heavy accents
of ground level talk.

Children playing in backyards
echo bits they catch; re-energize
them with laughter, toss
them multiplying upward

Where summer thunder clouds
discard their storm's intent;
take on aureoles, trail blue
and fuchsia across the evening sky.

At Blue Ridge

Under the hemlock
the rain is rationed. The crown
first drinks, then bathes,
spilling bubbles down slipping tips.
Surface tension strains, yields.

Green atoms bend their loads earthward
and inside the dark
circumference, the trunk tent pole
channels creeks.

These disappear under last year's
needled island
made moist in perfect proportion
for memories of other broken droughts
to grow.

Harvest

How fragilely
as from out of season snows
the bean discards its flower base
and takes the risk and grows.

While tomato paints its urgent red
against the parent vine
to shine through glass on pantry shelves
as summer art in winter time.

Earth Zero

Earth zero is not the plane under my feet;
it lies below; it floats on the upper edge of the water table;
it follows the contours of the earth at that depth,
climbing the highest mountains
submerged below continental shelves to dry rock
cooling still from magma.

It stretches above me into the stratosphere
there where oxygen disappears at the thinnest layer
maybe riding tops of cumulous clouds,
towering thunderheads a boundary of ups and downs
of an astronomical roller coaster dipping here, climbing there
then plunging to compress and play a game of sorts
with layered cirrus,
switching on magnetic fields in wild display.

In this space I live, feeling the majesty of such distances,
knowing where I walk, fly, swim is important
to all that lies beneath me, knowing
that my foreshortened stretch of finger
has pointed energy to every other border,
there, above me, beyond, beneath, beside me,
where, if I persist
I could only die…an adventurer in precious space,
from earliest time embroidered with inscriptions from stars;
auras from borealis coloring jeweled scarves
evident still in geologic strata,
edges of not ground zero, but ground everything
real, insistent, tipping always to the positive
away from zero. To something. Never nothing.

Dogwood

Sometime, somewhere
in our winter's sleeping,
snow fell,
took root.

Gathered now to blossoms
it crowns the darkness
hovering under the dogwood.

Pansies

Do not lightly take this road
look neither
left
    nor
        right

one could so easily go drunk

                        on blue

die
                                    of all

                                        that yellow

Darien in Spring

At Darien in spring, Azalea
is the common denominator of pretty.
How pretty equals only how many.
Not related to the house
in whose yard they bloom,
not the variety—
Just mass.

Colors blend brilliantly,
subtly hybridize from blossom to blossom
to say nothing of leaps from shrub to shrub.

Rows of them throb
around fishing folks'
shotgun tarpaper-covered shacks;
grandly illumine back roads.

Swirled in pink,
cotton candy colors dawn
and all day mauves and fuchsias
denigrate sun.

At dark, shadows run to purple.

For weeks we surfeit on beauty,
stagger under weights of wealth
unknown to us where winters
are too cold for pink;
offer in recompense
richness of hemlock, fir.

When we leave Darien for home again,
crossing first low terraces
of ancient coastal plains
our hearts respond
get on line
with familiar arithmetic
of base mountain.

After the Storm

Three birds:
one cardinal
a titmouse
a chickadee
who had fed well all day
on food strewn generously
on the other side of the kitchen window-pane
froze in night's sudden blizzard;
after the melt lay scattered.

A single dogtooth violet
sheltered by steps
had its say about the unexpected.

I take the ratio to heart:
three birds for one violet
seems a hard bargain.

One more time I am glad
not to be in charge, unable
to read omens.

Just know
there had been
briefly coexisting
a string of song,
a thread of color
pulling over the edge of necessity
toward happiness.

Surveying Trillium

Where trillium grows, we walk the line
to see if it is his, or mine.
Sessile abundant, nodding rare
and property rights being what they are

I look above to search the sky
to see on which side each may lie
and hope an arc of some degree
declares they all belong to me.

Less comfort found in clouds that shift
than in the leaves which form a drift
of cover bracing trillium stem
which says but few belong to him.

A need to put all science by
in service to my greedy eye
informs my very careful foot
to move regarding every root

That hides from the surveying rod
to lose itself in mossy sod,
erasing angles as one should
that cut through trillium in the wood.

H A I K U

Cardinals

Fly now from scolding...

But winter color will shout

just who stole rose hips

Ready

A row of oak trees

like the dancers' open fans

waits for wind music.

Utsukushi Desu

In far distances

snowing daisies crown mountains

...Dream of Fujisan

Overture

You would have to know how the land lies:
a former pond bed, filled by decades of slow detritus,
still divided by a narrow branch bearing the England family name,
not even a yard wide, slopes away from what was once
rock reinforced banks, offering uneasy footing, but subject
to sky and surrounding trees.

Along the edges storms have pruned the forest of all tall pines,
poplars, and underbrush.

So this morning what I was given
were sentinel shadows stretching over wet bottomland
in long lines like the music teacher drew on the chalkboard
with her magic device.

Five lines in one sweep of hand if chalk
did not fall from wire springs, or break from dramatic flings
done over shoulder as she recited spaces
F A C E and lines E G B D F
and we repeating, her chorus of pipers, recognizing rhythm,
a sing-song strange alphabet.

Lines the sun drew as it waked trees were fuzzy,
but absolutely recognizable.
Space between treble and bass courtesy of a white pine
fallen up-hill.

As line projections completed from side to side in the copse,
the orchestra flew on stage; bird shadows played from note to note,
perching briefly for eighths, flying upward and whirling downward.
What crescendos, glissandos!
Always overtures, da capos!

Whatever of dark hint came as bass echoing from sink and laundry
drumming duty forte, Forte, Fortissimo dragged me from window
audio visual staging. I would not see/hear the full score, finale.

Another day, perhaps at sunset.

Horses in Snow

Horses crowd the pasture corner, gray,
while yesterday before the snow
they loomed so white, carriage matched
to take the tourists down our country road.

Now that snow has bleached the leafless boles
and given froth to pine and every laurel bush
color assumptions prove just that:
they were not white, but on the way to being.

And we the watchers not precise until
the winter weather forced us
to another way of seeing.

Nothing But Rain

Nothing but rain can do what the rain does.

Hoses cannot reach high enough to gentle down
to tops of trees, let trickles bathe between the plates of bark,
run rivulets down vertical troughs, reach ground slowly.

Nor do they run around the clock; with some prescience
falling early, early in the dawn
and coming with their say
they mean to stay positively, absolutely
all day.
On the roof the message strong, clear,
it is okay to move yourself as slowly as you wish;
from window to window; open the door to smell
its firm intent.

You have permission to take time out...
out from anything,
especially any nagging chore
and gaze your soul-full,
worshipping moisture.

At Nasawaddox

I. Siege

They were disguised at first,
playful sport for patron gods.
In time each chrysalis stretched
and one day they birthed themselves.

She the humanist.
He all science.

They should have known better
but they still went camping together.

For fires he dragged from marsh,
beach, or cedar windbreak
logs still moist, rich habitat
for slugs, earthworms, pill bugs,
a variety of ants, would throw
resident life with log across coals
and Armageddon's hell fire
only a skein of smoke away.

Frantically she stooped;
with both hands lifted away
whatever was most in danger.
Ants deflected in frenzy;
worms were more difficult.

A smell of singe floated on the air.
Time had to be called for smudging
braids back over her shoulders.

His irritation grew: "That's stupid,"
he spit; "If they finished
a normal lifetime here,
every one would be dead by morning."

"But not in my fire," she shouted,
stooping in renewed panic
for all civilian casualties.

II. Dawn

Here on this spit of eastern shore,
coils of mist garner upward from marsh;
obscure however well-intentioned sun.

Edges of murk test climates of two oceans,
fly upward as feather detached
from pillow of gray and darker plumps
on the world's rim—fall in downdrafts;
exchange gray energies.

Gray pulses everywhere:
we inhale it,
give it back—
both oceans
full from silt,
salt-gray,
darker
than ashes where it roils
from water to air.

Because our clocks
declare sun has risen
we too rise—
farmers plow dull fields
as others go to offices;
children to school—gray
fading bright cardigans
meant to identify
fogged bodies as they board
shrouded buses.

Shadows have banded
our world forearm-high
before sun puts tentative fingers
through our weighted atmosphere;
begins to make real again
what we have dealt with by remembering.

As light emerges here
one handful at the time, inland
by fifteen degrees, friends

entirely too casual with such miracle
measure their six A.M. horizon;
immediately claim dawn.

III. Tern

Bird, go!

This plowed soil
dried to color
lighter than loam
to which the storm
threw you mocks beach.

Troughs undulated
behind yesterday's tractors
are rigid; no waves
lap here.

It is wind that foams
over windbreak edges, crests
cedar, pine, willow oak.
Their soughings
are not surf.

Your hormones heavy for planting
accelerate nesting to high gear
beyond caution that tomorrow
tractors come again,
follow the farmer's drive;
he, too, heavy; six thousand
pounds of seed urgent as yours
for hollows'
easy earth cover.

Driven by my own needs,
I am unprepared for you,
lack even a stone to throw,
throw my angry prayer
on the eastern shore wind.

Damn, damn you, bird, this is not the place.

Evolution

Bird is dinosaur made acceptable,
getting those slender legs,
and not content with new skin show,
taking to sky to really boast.

Still dinosaurs, extinct, lumber
across our nightmares
crush ancient landscapes
destroy egg of what he might have become.

All so long ago no one postulates
how the giants might have bellowed;
the poets had not yet arrived to record
and no one has thought to call the missing link
a missing sound.

Only the slow ages at work,
and one day in pre-history
a sound not heard before…
and more
and more
and song was born…
a new dimension.

I declare I do love birds
For such striving.

Plum Blossoms

A miracle overnight;
Black bark turned white.
Something urgent
Sought to spring;
Something silent
Thought to sing.

Silver Apricot

This gingko leaf
its design saved exactly
from the Jurassic until now
though more than once
nearly lost as contemporaneous
dinosaurs

was cultivated away from extinction
by ancient monks
blending botany prayers
with penitent labors
praising by planting
to preserve perfect bi-lobar grace
of leaves that looked like ferns
set dancing by merest murmur

until heavy with gold
in season they tumbled
to ruffled tiers skirting bole
showing how sparely it branched
while leaves lent
generous substance.

Keeping close watch
in sacred grounds
it was the monks who named them.

Honesty forbidding poetry
honoring science
they studied not full fruit
but beginning
rough clothed drupe
like lumpish green apricot
with suggestion of sheen
and then said:

Yin for *Silver*
and *Kyo* for *Apricot.*

A poorly tuned western ear
wounded consonants
renamed the tree
whose miniature fan
cools my fever

from weight
of so much alchemy.

Never So White

Never so white as now red,
the dogwood burns its way up the hill,
flames leaping as winds shear away
last leaves, bringing clusters of berries
stage center, myriads of tight bouquets
scarlet, orange, whatever color flame
wears from first catching
to last radiance, vanguard
sparks a fusillade exploding
against October blue, November gray.
When the fires die, bird and wind
having dissipated every trace,
and on the forest floor
leaves curl crisp,
memories of red multiply infinitely
until first snow, and then,
only then,
can we remember white.

The Certain Moment

A certain slant of dog hobble leaf
under rain, early
easing away
from night's storm
declared the season.

Autumn arrived exactly
when surface tension
disregarded
waxy slick green
slowed drops
ordering
a stately, legato procession
from stem to tip.

All day long
in recognition of the grand occasion
a second-hand very local rain
thus dripped from hundred foot poplars
under a sky turned clearest blue.

Wisteria

Wisteria is a color all its own,
not nearly purple, hardly lavender—
and the white, not white, but fading cream—

It smells that same luminous pale;
the smell, more provocative than real
of crepe paper costumes we wore;
skirts made from clumsily shaped leaves,
festoons of crinkly blossoms, burgeoning,
three dimensional as our mothers could make—
costumes as much on trial as performers
in Fourth Grade Spring Festival.

One must be careful in the wisteria dance;
the basting stitches might tear through
and a petal fall to the gymnasium stage floor

The way the March wind breaks
clusters from the captive pine
to splatter occasional soft color,
crepe paper smell, by the kitchen door.

Two For Renoir

I. The Bathers

Renoir tied in his sedan chair
painted dancers and swimmers;
called his picture of bathers
at Cagnes his best work.

He painted it with brushes
strapped to his wrist.
While his son and Grand' Louise
arranged linen between his clamped fingers,
and colored his palette,
models and river danced a mockery
of his prison.

Now it is we who are immobilized
before such careless grace,
the totally lighted motion in his prism.
The ineluctable holy beauty of flesh
dooms us to the irony.

One could cry *Piteous,*
Oh piteous, search
for a healing metaphor.

Perhaps the bones closed
on light he snared
one day, and gods were jealous.

In which case their error not to steal
what was stored of motion
in his marrow.
Wrist would be enough.

II. Renoir, Do Not Apply

The women at Cagnes
quit renting their houses
to Renoir. Mme Renoir
was prompt with *le location*
but when summer light
faded and the family returned
to L'Essayes near Paris, one by one
the housewives found tables,
chests, and once a marble mantelpiece
with their corners cut off.

Ah, cet homme Renoir!

Yes, he had carefully sanded the cuts smooth,
but still, *Quelle domage!*
your furniture not safe. What if he did paint
those beautiful women, those perfect children?

And then, he was never even sorry,
not a word in apology. He only gave you a lecture
on the danger of sharp corners.

The children's eyes...didn't you know
such a thing could blind one
and all that light gone forever?

Skink

When I released the pressure your head
burrowed spasmodically into an opening
not deep enough to let all of you in.

I knew you would die in slow pain,
but hadn't the stomach for digging you out
and ending it decently, having already
committed so indecent an act.

All day long you have dug at my consciousness;
your innocence its own kind of poison.

Circumstances exaggerated caution;
another like you plunging under prunings
I only wanted to gather for fireplace kindling
echoed children screaming "Copperhead!"

When your body writhed upward
I saw too late
your species' foreshortened legs
still running; the air unsubstantial.

Your disproportionate body recalled
embryos and newborns of my kind;
these overlaid your brown
and for a moment
you were all pink.
That was when
I would have saved you,
but already I had not.

It had been my choice; now my loss
of electric blues and greens in ribbons
across summer lighted stones
where copperheads have never come.

Weighing

How much does the earth weigh?
How much the stone inside?
Gneiss…schist, this questionable granite
lying on your breakfast table,
a crumb from the tons piled
out your back door, waiting
for you to pick up piece by piece
for your retaining wall.

How hard it must be for earth to turn such mass,
balanced as it is on not only polar axis
but some equatorial fulcrum also,
keeping it level in its orbital plane,
swinging up and down like children on a see-saw
and the see-saw on the merry-go-round.

I think so much weight drawn from quarries,
distributed without a thought as to what the earth can bear
would send the planet reeling on detour.

We are saved for the very short term
by the magnitude of its strainings toward light,
balancing against the immense heaviness
of connecting tilth; weightless love
having no specific gravity, no place on atomic scale
no mathematical equivalent,
no formula. Only the mystery.

In Re: Rhododendron

I. Barometer

Rhododendron is my barometer.
When cold is briskly bearable,
its stems resilient, the leaves brilliant mirrors—
not green, but fractiled prisms,
I need no sweater, or if so, only the lightest.

But when leaves curl,
hang stiff as frozen jeans
on country clothes lines, beware.

It is cold; inner energies protected by the guard cells
cannot compete forever. What once seemed tiers
of dancers' skirts, no longer held by hoops, now
fold over the mid vein.
It is pitiful to see how vulnerable the dancer,
no substance there, after all;
if touched there will be a breaking
where middle life-layers give way.

The epidermis cracks on either side
and on the ballroom floor among emerging violets
no rhododendron leaf lies flat;
in death still curling for something to hold to;
the thing that had held them together.

II. Mirror

My spirit body curves like leaves on the rhododendron,
when blizzard cold freezes the guard cells.
My edges shrink and pull backward
so that once straight surfaces, glossy with light
tighten.
There is nothing to hold me; nothing to hold to.
Nothing can warm; there is nothing to cuddle.
I shrivel, dry up for lack of something to hold,
like a lover,

like a small child.
There is no blanket that will do.

In the real forest,
between the layers of the leaves
the epidermis, the mesophyl and the other epidermis
closing the sandwich, top, middle, bottom,
the guard cells, the stoma, balance intake
and outflow of spongy heart necessities....

In such cold we too curve and medicine names a disease
osteoporosis...it sounds so reasonable; so explainable,
but the doctors do not know the medicine of the imagination;
do not know the shriving
of emptiness; the core removed; lover and child gone,
how we crispen as we try harder and harder to find something
for empty arms.

It Is at Least in Part the Wind

If you should marvel at the geography
of birds after summer doldrums,
long hiatus of flight,
torpid days' scant flutter,
purely local,

then

catapulted

departure,

do not discount
the everywhere love
of air for stir,

the winds, too,
listless over dog days
under August heat,
remember wings
along now slack sleeves
drooping north to south,

cry,

their innate directions
never contravened:

This way,
come,
fly here.

Let me not to the marriage of true minds
Admit impediments. Love is not love
Which alters when it alteration finds,
Or bends with the remover to remove.

From *Sonnet 116*
William Shakespeare

V. A Few For Love

An Appalachian Woman Counts the Ways

I love you how garden green things growing
each tendril where to reach everything knowing.

I love you every bird its own path winging
over creek sandy shadows all stones singing.

How I love you in cold is coal orange burning
in dark night to light momently turning.

In spring how ferns their fronds unwinding
beckon to jug-plant children finding.

In autumn how heavy crows corn-shocked calling
and how out in the wintered woods all snow falling.

The Heart Tends to Its Business

I. Codicil

I party of the first part
who consigned to you
party of the second, my heart,
by virtue of your having seen,
what I was, or might have been,

Promise I will heal in time though hard beset,
if time lasts—and will be validated yet
by what birds wrote upon the sky,
what wind whispered, what stone taught of pain,
then comforted to laughter by a freshening rain;
too wise to dream beyond the fire
to which we sacrificed desire,
heedless of the anomaly
that fire gives back to breathing air
every atom burning there.

II. Receipt

Such music as stream and birds afford
cadenced from mysteries you heard
and translated to me by word
I doubly debtor then

and aureoled light
in which to move
in orbits toward the rim of love
giving on drunken undreamed space
whose cosmos whirled about your face.

Gratefully acknowledged:
hearing seeing,
these gifts of knowing.

Beyond,
in innocent surprise,
treasured more than music flowing
the look with which you held me
somehow, so deep,
so safe within your eyes.

Had We Together Known Red Bougainvillea

How wanton our love beneath such roseate air,
passion bleeding from heaven...
such voluptuous plentitude
weighting our cells,
finding delaying routes to earth
through our bodies,
slowing the cyclical return
lest like too much sun, too long,
it turn the earth to stone.

And we offering gladly to dance
between that radiance and the grass,
our shadows diminishing by just so much
the color, the heat pulsing our veins
and we become no more, no less,
than tremulous leaves caught in earth's throbbing.

What we knew together was fir;
austere, forbidding, against northern sky,
in winter condemning us with white death,
in summer deadly still, dark green spires
addressing what might otherwise be heaven
with moral rectitude.

Had we together known red bougainvillea
nothing could have saved us.

Letter Home

Did I write to you, as promised about the beach at Ju?
That Sunday, when the boat found its own way
to where trees rooted in sheered rock behind the narrow sand?
Where my party left me, and where I climbed the impossible tree,
alone, until the three children came, pointing, laughing,
daring choices of more and more dangerous climbs?

I hear them across needled spaces as they call each other, me:
"Otomodachi, abunai, Obasan, abunai!"
"Hey, Buddy, watch out; Honorable lady, be careful."
And we repeat our *abunais* until we understand. "Look how foolish
we are; perhaps not us kids, but the American lady must be crazy."

Sliding to where dwindling limbs will exactly bear our weights,
we ride the wind as it confronts the cliff, explodes rainbows skyward.
I become lost in a world where past, present, future fuse.
Without ambiguity I emotionally understand the unified field.

As my party returns, I want to hide, but decorum prevails. I descend,
and the children follow, scattering cones in sporadic tumbles.
I move toward the boat; the children to a wider beach,
where they perhaps, only perhaps, hear my compulsive shout:

"Abunai, abunai, abunai, desu yo!"
Careful, Careful, one must be careful. One could forget today.

Did you get this letter? I never found it in your saved things.
What I really need to know, now, even now is:
If you got it, did it make you smile?

Betrothal Gift

I think one day
you will walk meadows;
the grass be comfortably
not too low...tall enough
for your free hand to brush,
winnow fragments, scatter seed,
the other holding your beloved's.

The free swinging also for picking
when you come to the edgings the flowers
bordering low forest shrubs.

These will be the colors of all palettes.
Lavenders of Meadow Queen, purple
of Joe Pye Weed. Cardinal flowers
will flash fire bolts and yellows sedately
bloom on Susans and Jerusalem Artichokes.

Where springs have left deep moisture
despite whatever droughts,
Jewel Weeds will still feed hummingbirds.
Yes, I have seen this late into October.

The samples you gather and show to each other
you will carry home, stick in a glass jar
on the kitchen window sill
to save what they will of magic
caught in autumn sun.

Lies

Should I decide to say your eyes were blue
not brown, imperfect after all, that you
lacked grace in bearing; that unruly hair
you brushed from forehead had no charm, that there
was in your speech no music, no delight,
no warmth in touch; if I deny that sight
of you was heaven, swear that I could live
a million years without you, never give
a thought to your keen laughter, see your length
along my mountain path, discover strength
to look away, swear men like you are free
for taking, much, oh much too dull for me—
If all of this—yet someone say your name,
all lies collapse; your eyes are brown again.

So Very

Can you recall
at all being merry?
So very?

When all it took
was a look
to beguile
a smile
in a nano while
then being extravagantly, madly glad?
hysterically, unrestrainedly glad?

And sad
was a word
we only heard?

Do you remember
a little the weather
we made together?

For ease from pain
a tin-roof rain?

When to be fed
was a cup of tea
from sassafras root
and Juneberry fruit?

Was there a warning of any kind
from subtle wind—
a change of form
to miniscule storm
besieging your mind
before placidity became your style?

When just barely for you would never do.
For you just barely catapulted to very.

For you it could never
be merely
just barely
but again and always
and surely be very.

(For you just barely
must never do.)

Repeat after me,
say it strong, dear,
and clearly:

"We never lived barely!
We always loved very,
alively awarely,
so very most very."

Taxonomy

The botanist's wife wanted to speak mountain,
know intimate granny-given flower names
to sing—make mantras. Sometimes their music
drowned the Latin on her husband's tongue.

His names stiff, dentate, pricklier than thorn
serrated the audial air—the ones she chose
downy as *foam flower* floated on *baby's breath.*

Prunella Canadensis, Mchx, he planted syllables
carefully—Oh *heart's balm* she would sigh.

Yucca wounded her imagination in ways
no *Spanish Bayonet* could punish flesh—
Better than both when in bloom was *Canterbury Bells*
their ivory sculptures pointing the path for pilgrims.

Recoiling from *Shrankia,* it was *sensitive plant*
she stroked to sleep, whose mauve powder puff
she waved about her face.

At times humor betrayed her, made hybrid metaphors.
The seldom unruly children she might report
on a day gone-to-seed as having been *Daucus carota*
and ignore a house in *wild carrot* disarray
to stuff fruit jars full of *Queen Anne's Lace.*

To tease, would ask the botanist
if there being a *Lady Lupine* might there be
a *Lord,* and if so, had Tchaikovsky hearing
Waltz of the Flowers imagined them?

The botanist's wife learned with requisite pain
about confrontations at the interface,
saw plants in either colony divided
by a line precise as Greenwich
grow puny as they stood their ground,
could not discern if such frail ranks

should retreat or advance,
learned that mutations rooted best
in rich compromise, practiced for a day
when she could end a walk with scholarly comment.

"That *Euonymous* over at the old house place
is lovely now. Is it the *Americana*?"

The botanist's wife knew she had a long way
to go, when in that same fantasy the botanist
looked deep in her eyes,
proclaimed them more *bluet* blue
than *Houstonia* could ever say before answering:

"Oh, yes, *Americana*—in fruit now, you see
why local women named it *Strawberry Bush*,
but I like best its other name, the one
you call it, '*Heart-bursting-with-love*.'"

If Ever I Should Lose My Sight

If ever I should lose my sight
one thing I would not have to study:
I think I would remember light.

Having known you in a field of white
I could recall its folds around your body
If ever I should lose my sight.

How to forget in such a plight
what one has learned so well already?
I think I would remember light

As you defining day from night
and by such surety hold steady.
If ever I should lose my sight

I might be given yet, just might,
for keeps, some glow from all that's pretty—
I think I would remember light.

While small gods do their works of spite
large ones compensate with pity.
If ever I should lose my sight
I will remember you as light.

The East Wind Keeps My Cove in Care

The east wind keeps my cove in care.
It brings the rain.
I shelter with my true love there.

When sun is more than field can bear
And song is silent in the grain
The east wind keeps my cove in care.

When wedded are the earth and air
Wet draperies close around our lane.
I shelter with my true love there.

While others search the sky with prayer
For time to mow the hay again
The east wind keeps my cove in care.

Outside the storm makes great affair:
Inside, wet dark shrouds window pane.
I shelter with my true love there.

Who have forgotten love, beware
Against such blessing to complain.
The east wind keeps my cove in care.
I shelter with my true love there.

Blue

Twice I have known blue
whatever it is that lingers blue
beyond measurable wavelengths
whatever it is that contracts the heart
rearranges rhythm after breath catches—

Once I thought blue hyperbole
resided only in violets
knew fields so lush
one could argue the world was upside-down
and walk topsy-turvy through sky.

Then I knew that I had seen blue
boiled and strained like
feathers dipped in a dyeing vat
spread on peacocks to dry.

So in flower and feather
have I known blue but twice
yet only the third time charms.
For this I dive through cataracts
to swim again
in the once taken-for-granted
sky full miracle
in your eyes.

Now

O my love,
wake,
stars are blooming
on Hamby Mountain.

Already
petals catch
in ground cover.

Such capricious light
we can float in crystal.

Others we will gather
with long stems
for your favorite vases.

For these
I will climb hemlocks,
pull branches low
for you to choose.

Hurry now
while night
still shows the way.

Waiting

Mon coeur, mon amour, mon bien aimé
Quand le printemps
Oui, mon coeur
Quand le printemps
Oui

My heart, my love, beloved
When spring,
Yes, my heart
When Spring
Yes

We

Watershed

There are things to remember about this day;
the house, the garden, and by the garden the river.
The music of the flute floating, the clarinet
clear indeed upon the mountain air.
And the river…
remember the river
in full orchestra playing its counterpoint
of water fingering stone.

Such a watershed this day; the long dreamed
merging of privately wandered paths, beyond
our knowing, always converging toward confluence
of the many rains, making numerous creeks, branches…
even the return to the earth
through warm-to-hot mornings of earliest dew;
the melting of frost in narrow meadows, the crack of ice
from trees, the melting of snow…all luring us to follow,
follow the watershed.

Now pledged together, facing upstream,
where like the river your life's geography
takes on more intricate patterns,
and the water on stone faithfully playing its counterpoint,
and you smile and remember the clarinet clear on air,
and the flute floating over the water
that makes boundary for the garden
and the garden wraps the house
where you announced yourself to your beloved.

Did it Matter That Time, That Cup of Coffee?

Did it matter that your hands
were delicate around the cup,
the cup of coffee, made especially for you...
with chicory, memorial from our far separate
childhoods, marked forever by frugality.

Did it matter that you poured the cream
so carefully, skimmed from last night's milk,
a treat because your milk-cows were dry.
Such things touched upon in the conversation.

Did it matter that you looked across the cup,
your fingers so beautiful, your eyes lighted
with warmth of kettle steam, talk, and chicory coffee.
Simplest of things.

Did it matter that your eyes, as did mine,
said more than words would dare;
neither would speak first, challenge fate
to destroy what was frugally ours.

When there was not enough coffee, poor women
harvested chicory...shredded roots, put them to dry
and boiled alone or with remains of coffee beans.
The harvest was spare, enough at a time, though only barely.
Just enough to see one through another day.

Women like me who would marry men like you,
who early learned what was enough;
enough, though only barely,
enough to see us through another day.

And leave cups warm from touch of beautiful hands,
and the words minimal, safe for whatever ears:
The coffee was so good. So good seeing you.
Hate to go. Have to. By By.

What did it matter, all of it? To ask *what*? to *measure*
such incident will always remain impossible. What matters
is that *it mattered,*
it mattered.

All of it mattered.

Beyond Words

after
you have
listened to my words
be quiet with me
still listen
please
to my silence

I would write on the door post WHIM. I hope it is somewhat better than "whim" at last, but we cannot spend the day in explanation.

From *Self Reliance*,
Ralph Waldo Emerson

VI. Some Mischief

C'est La Vie

C'est la vie, he said to me.
La vie, I said.
Not *say*, but *c'est la vie*, I mean.
I said it once, I said.

A game of fractured repartee?
Not if you say *C'est*,
Then you say *C'est repartie.*
But *Repartie* seemed wrong to me.

A silly game we played a while—
Quite inexpensive, words;
A frown until we understood
And could afford a smile.

But weary grows the intellect
With language only toy,
And that is when we each could speak
Our lingua franca...full of joy.

All that was needed but *Adieu*
Adieu to *Toi,*
                    Adieu to *Moi.*

Conjugating To Be

I am, you *Are*   *!ERA uoy, ma I*

I am, you are I am also?   !era EW !eW

Over there, someone. He, She, is. Aren't they?

I am, you are, he is, she is, we are!

!ERA EW ERA EW. si ehs, si eh ton era eW

More *We Ares*?   *!erom, erom, erom, era eW*

Two they ares be one we are?   *!seY, seY,*

I am
You are
He/she is.
We are, we ones, weuns are.
He, she, they, thoseones, thoseuns are.
You ones, youuns, youse guys, youall, y'all are.
We are you are they are
because I am and you am and he, she, am and they am also.

Da Capo
(Conversation at Darien, Georgia)

"Won't all that fern kill the tree?"

I don't know,
you will have to ask the tree.

"Well, if you will be interpreter."

I don't speak tree either;
I could try my Spanish on the moss.

Which, after all, didn't speak Me,
who fell back on bronzed words
announcing age of church
shaded by oak.

And I think it will not be fern
but age and weight of church
on roots that kills the tree,
my faith however, certain
that when tree goes, fern
will still resurrect in rain.

"You think oak and fern
might be carrying on
their own conversation—
oak telling fern what to do?

I don't know,
You will have to ask the tree.

Days of Our Lives

Days of the week have names;
then they change to numbers
in a group that has names, *months*,
whose names change to numbers
in a *year* that has numbers
until there are ten.

Then there is a word again, a *decade*,
and ten of them make a word again
a *century.*

And ten times ten of them again
and a hundred centuries
make a new word *millennium.*

All of these built on spaces we repeat:
monday, tuesday,
wednesday, thursday, friday,
saturday, sunday.

And these we can further reduce:
dawn, mid-day, and evening,
and those back to component hours,
minutes, seconds, their micros
and nanos blinking on the micro-waves.

All of them having names;
all of them having first names only.
The family name is Life.
It's soubriquet, Time.

Excuse me, Sir, Ma'am, Miss,
Can you tell me what time it is?

Grandchildren,

Your science is usually better than mine.
However, you must listen while I educate you
about the recent lunar eclipse.

I fear from former conversations
that you see this marvel as though a lens cover
were sliding across the end of a telescope barrel
and somewhere a magic-lantern show astronomer
were in charge of one flat disc moving over another.

This is not at all the case.

Do not neglect that we are globular,
madly spinning and orbiting, as is our moon.
and we keep right on spinning as it does, and as the sun
during the entire process.

Imagine the enormity of it all!
Imagine the mathematics!
Do not think for one moment
this is something to demonstrate
with flashlights and three beach balls.

There is more.

All the above being true,
it follows that as the sun
throws our spinning shadow
there is one precise moment,
just one, when the leading edge,
one measurable shadow curve of longitude
bites into the light of the spinning moon.
Then, that longitude disappears into the back
of the shadow. Imagine how black the black
of the back side of a shadow!

Are you with me still?

Then, imagine you happen to be
at that longitude, you have climbed

a tree, the tallest on your mountain,
leaned eastward as far as gravity allows,
stretched your arms, your fingers
as far as possible and waved
exuberant greetings.

Then, would it not be you, your hand
making that fuzzy, amorphous
first piercing of the full-moon light?

Could it not be you?
Was it not I, there in newspapers
in the soft-toned photographs?
(Chances improve if you hold
your tree top through fifteen degrees
of spin. That is one hour, kids,
A new longitude moving over
every fractured nano-second.)

And if you tell me
I cannot prove it happened
like that last Wednesday night
and into Thursday morning,
I will use your own practiced logic
and say: "You can't prove it didn't,
and besides,
if I didn't, why was I so dizzy
afterwards
if not from all that spinning.
clinging,
waving?"

I invite you to join me here when it happens again.
The tree will be even taller
and we will really hang out.

Hat

It is a Mary Cassatt
kind of hat.
Pink, not the smoky red
of Charpentier, courtesy of Renoir,
under which one would float from room
to room on any *soir*
(ée)
as others ask who is the la
dy so newly in bloom?

It deserves high vaulted roof
of museums, cathedrals, elegant stem
in proportion to brim
enthralling proof
this hat
a veritable Cassatt
whim.

Never at all for regular Sunday
church affairs.
Involuntary stares
will deflect, re-route prayers.

Lesser chapeaux
would slide from head after head
of those in shame from wearing red.
Pink, pink, why didn't one know?

And rose, spun of chiffon from air
would not, could not, bloom but there.
And blooming, never fade,
having been of rose-dream made.

To live *on, at, that hat,*
which, take it from me
if it didn't exist
is exactly the hat
that Mary Cassatt
would see.

Jonquils

Nancy, Dear Nancy,
do you count your jonquils just now blooming
as you leave for work early, before heavy light?
Don't dismiss this as a silly question.
I have known very well some close in the family
who have done that.

On her behalf I would say she was really counting
to think when there would be enough
for two bouquets. One for herself, one for another.
That needed at least ten or twelve.

Forsythia fills out such a bouquet nicely,
and if there is white spirea, a mix of that—
and if the jonquils are long stemmed,
one could get by with, say, three.

But oh, the first one! How many telephone calls
have begun: "I just now found my first jonquil in bloom!"

Back to yours, the matter of concern here.
Your yard just seems right for everything.
And already there are dozens, dozens of yellow cups
spilling temptation down hill to me. So, yes, I did go.

At first I thought to get only three, and those
where you would never miss them. *(Unless you count.
Nancy, do you count? Jonquils, Nancy?)*

Every time I made a choice, Doubt came calling.
This, this is the one *she* would pick, exactly because
no one would miss it here. You think she doesn't know
where every bulb in this yard is?

I tried after that to be doubly discreet. Way up on top
of the hill. And down by the wood pile where *He* kept
stacking the red oak. I think *green red oak* is a hoot!
Sounds like a ready made Christmas tree, don't you think?

Like *He* said, the bulbs came right on up; several bunches
there in full bloom...exactly where your car lights
when you come in late would show you where you had left them,
safely, just at dawn. Couldn't pick those, Nancy.

Finally came home, though with three pieces of green red oak
for the kitchen stove, picked four of my own struggling jonquils;
do not look out the window toward the exposed emptiness.

But Nancy, a thought did strike me, seriously. If I were applying
for a job and was being questioned as to my honesty something like
did I steal paper and pencils and pens (there are such nice ones now)
from the office, etc, etc, etc, and had to say if I maintain my morality
only some of the time, most of the time, or all of the time,
I would say, oh, all of the time...unless...unless, Nancy,
Do you think jonquils count?

Mother, I'm Afraid
(Sins venial and mortal)

Mother, I'm afraid
that I have not lived exactly
as you would have wished.

I have remained something of a dreamer
(My father's side of the family?)
and delayed the dreams until they disappeared.
I said good-by to the church—not the one we knew
from your teaching, but the one that it became;
once ordered a Mormon Missionary
from my house. MOTHER!
you would not have believed that scene—
he shook the dust from my carpet from his feet.

I do take comfort in the grounding you gave.
For small virtues, I have sheltered a few homeless,
though never enough; fed more. Always I have thrown
last of the dishwater on flower beds
for birds and worms; my deepest sense of sin
remains the wasting of food when any living thing
is hungry.

Always when moving, I have cleaned
the house I moved from (yes, did do the windows)
and passed that down to the grandchildren you never knew.
They respect the history of that obligation.

You would not like it that at thirty-five a long pent-up anger
released itself in a profane vocabulary. I learned not only
to curse, but to do it well. Mother, it seemed good,
and I continued to do it on many occasions, though now
at many years over your age when you died,
I need this less.

I definitely came to believe that sex is not a sin.

On sum, I have not lived up to you
in spite of niggardly grasping for redemption.

But there is a last list.
The milk bottle was never left on the table
during a meal, no matter how tired I was,
and though catsup has stayed in its bottle, Mother,
I never never never served mayonnaise from a jar.

Resumé

Once she was not: then she was.
Once she could not swim: then she did.
For her very life, through the dark canal.

Once she had not cried: then she did.
She did a thousand things she had never done before.

First of all she sucked in air, then warm liquid.
She did this over and over, so it must have felt good
inside her mouth throat stomach bowel
where it soured and passed through—
A mess this was too—into what ever caught it.

One day she was able to direct this into a pot.
Around her there was great joy and clapping of hands
as people who loved her gazed upon the marvel.

As this was happening in the meantime
she flexed and was flexed and wrinkles stretched smooth.

And in this same meantime she heard language
and began to imitate what she heard.

After years of this she learned to draw these words
and direct them to say something that she alone controlled.
She hoped as with the pot there would be clapping of hands.

One day she finished learning the word drawing
and saying lessons and wanted to show others
how to do this. And she did. She did.

One day she did not know about sex: then she did.
One day she did not like what she knew: then she did.
One day she thought she knew it all: then she didn't.

One day she thought since she knew
she could be improved, she should have
some little other selves
on whom to practice improvement so she did.

She did not know they would rebel
and be their own selves.

When she knew this she watched them
with great love and interest and let them
improve her wherever they could.
They did their best. They did. They did.

Again in the meantime she flexed and all sorts
of things and persons and circumstances flexed her,
so that where once flexings had smoothed her
everything was now wrinkled.

One day she had never quit doing: then she quit doing.
Again warm soft things were all she craved.
She sucked at air even more noisily,
sometimes through tubes, and food through straws
as all she wanted in her mouth, throat, stomach, bowel.

Again it did not matter where the liquid or solid mess
expelled itself. Some days she still directed it
into a pot and as before persons who loved her
and complete strangers congratulated her and clapped hands.

One day she thought she would swim again.
Absolutely before long she was going to take
the deepest breath of all time and plunge straight
into that dark canal and get to the other end,
the one she must have intuited at the beginning—
else why so frightening the first time?

Once she had not known the interrupted swim
made a word: L I F E!
Now she knew
that life and death were waters
sweetly mixed; a single stream swirling though dark
and light also.

Once she was:
Then she was not.

Soap Opera

In the beginning,
perhaps on the ninth day
after mankind on the eighth day
had invented MONEY
an under princeling,
kin of deposed satan
most likely, invented a number
of soap operas.

Not knowing how man would
obey the multiplying order,
he didn't create enough
so that sometimes the same opera
had to fall to more than one person-to-be,
at least two to one.
Usually these two would be married
to each other.

Trapeze

I tight-rope walk on changing latitudes.
Under my feet they sag
as I balance against new places.

If they break
I could plunge
all the way
to Antarctica
and at the acceleration
of thirty-two feet per second, per second
slide off the planet.

I rejoice to have learned
enough in Physics 101
to know a healthy fear,
try to behave nicely
in strange towns.

"Poetry is what you write when you can't say what you want to say any other way."

with permission
Chris Nalley,
eighth grade student,
White County, Georgia, Middle School

VII. Ars Poetica

Bill Moyers & Co., Care of Power of the Word

What do you mean
attacking my heart with your words?
Their images drag it through gravel sharp
emergency exits of my mindscape;
penetrate its cellular interfaces
where until now space was so carefully,
molecularly allotted.

Its arteries of thought restricted,
narrowed with your word plaque
so that it swells with a visceral swell
to absorb the infusion;
if it explodes its justified returned fire
will brand you with your own cloned scars.

Nothing will be safe.
You will feel again the Black
you made it be: the Indian, the Eskimo,
the Poor-White in Piney Woods Mississippi
in the middle of Chicago in the L. A. Jail.

The prescribed arteriogram shows
vulnerable bundles laboring to accommodate
the faces you put there; the fluid
battleground established by your invasion;
a civil war of unprecedented proportions.

Blips on the screen tend to straight lines,
confirm the trauma; threat of death
from the pain loaded on your words.

Dining In

Dear Pat,
I ate your poem
for breakfast this morning.

It was so appetizing,
centered
on the yellow placemat,
bold black ink,
white paper.

Who could ask
for more beguiling
decor?

Oh, the biting in!
Everything crisp,
al dente,
dear friend.

Requiring
just enough effort
to challenge digestion—

Thank you.

Mrs. McDonald
(Caveat Magistra)

At eight I knew death as the ultimate
looming punishment and with pure
vindictive glee privately celebrated
when Mrs. McDonald died.

It was exactly what she deserved
for having called my mother to school
to tell her I could not possibly have written
the poem I had written.

It was about tulips and had predictable
labored rhyme. The rhythm however
was perfect—that was what she could not believe
she said, as I sat there
multiplying hatred to match wound.

I was almost caught up by fourth grade
when Mrs. McDonald died.

It took some years of my own sinning
to teach me forgiveness for our mutual
misinterpretations. I am wiser now;
not so much in matters of how
and why we die, as in the strange
species of ruin that may lie
in reading, or writing,
a poem.

At Susan's

I gathered the forsythia stems
in the dark; there was not a minute
to get a flashlight
if I were to be on time
for poetry reading.

I knew the bushes well;
broke them easily,
a stiff handful.

Just as easily Susan
went to her dark kitchen,
picked a pitcher by exacting feel.

She brought into the lighted room
a completed mutual sculpture.
Its imprecise image
against the white wall
beguiled us across seasons:
shadow swollen buds
for a moment bloomed.

When they proclaim their actual yellow hope
they will be no more beautiful
than as we saw them then,
putting aside poetry,
seeing prophecy,
recreating Eden.

Collisions

Where the heart pushes upward
and brain goes down to merge,
one or the other having dream of a word,
there might be a fibrillation, something not painful:
a sense of thrill, as corpuscular accommodations
race; the flow coming from left brain, and mid-placed heart
to pulse across breast bone, up clavicle, to shoulder,
down nerves, through ligaments to right hand, which has known
the while to pick up pencil, pen, or as with our ancients,
a stick for sand.

Whether first or second, the brain has to deal with the word.
Ensuing connections are why it loses dream substance
so perfectly heard, modified by all obstructions. The right
ear felt a rushing in labyrinth as phrases hurtled through narrowing
channels between reality and the still resisting dream.
Nothing can stop the erosion.

While translations go from body to paper, so much is lost:
Heart-birds have flown away; brain ferns unfolded, their fronds
already spotted; the curl of rose wilted;
the little waterfall slackened.

As with shapes, colors have defied capture: only heart
and mind realize how much they faded in the instants.

So subtle each change, but so momentous...
we cannot remember what it is we should be mourning.

In Storage

When Susan returned the bowl
I had taken to her
filled with snapped Kentucky Wonders,
she had covered the bottom with words
typed on bits of paper
like the beans, of varying lengths,
though mostly uniform,
long as thumb
for casual measuring.

Her harvest offered me beans in German,
Italian, French; Aphorisms clever and wise,
adjectives, adverbs, evoking planting, growth
and taste, for relish with canned green snaps
or dried Leather Britches.

I think under their plastic wrap
these words will keep for a long time;
nourishment preserved for the day
when more forgetful than now, I struggle
with my deepest hunger—ravenous longing
for match of sound to meaning,
the perfect word; Word Incarnate; not the one
my clever alter-ego substitutes,
sometimes even beginning
with the same letter as the one that lies
out there on the tip of a vine
whose tendrils I trace to the roots
but cannot reach.

Perhaps then I will take down
the brown oven-proof bowl
and re-compute a word still crisp
in Susan's memory.
Be fed.

To the Young Poets

I will forgive your being young
as you, my being old
if from our words we shape a song.

Be it ill or well begun
be it timid song or bold
I will forgive your being young.

Between what's meant and what is sung
there's fuel still against the cold
if from our words we shape a song.

The words your questions thrive among
I scarce afford to scold.
I will forgive your being young.

For you will move where I have gone;
echoes from old scores unfold
if from our words we shape a song.

Since time tricks all before he's done,
changing plot as our story is told,
I will forgive your being young
if from our words we shape a song.

Poetry Night at Schroeder's New Deli Courtyard

Court convenes at seven P.M. on fourth Tuesday evenings
of May, June, July, August, but only if it doesn't rain.

The jury volunteers; the accused never challenge.
Appearing pro se, the defendants one by one present their briefs.
Frenziedly scribbled addenda call for expository asides,
deprecating gestures, disclaimers.

No matter how the speakers protest, the jury is not fooled;
recognizing the poseur confiding so genuinely how it is
with that other woman, that other man...always
the situations are oblique; personal pronouns
risk contempt of court.

From the so-cool recitations listeners delineate the acid
inside-out entrail anguish and to whom it belongs.
They know exactly who got raped and who paid for the abortion.
They know who sobbed when the door slammed behind which lover.
They know who screamed Nigger and who belonged to the KKK.
They know who died and they know who mourns.

And I, the foreman declare to the judge that we find
the defendants though guilty as hell,
not punishable for perjured identifications
because of pain already paid.

My own brief is postponed for a less crowded calendar.

To the Poet

I awoke to
a world of
rationed words. We
were each to
have three point
zero zero six.

A dream so
precise sent me
to frantic arithmetic
full of millions
for long division.

I confess I
cheated; threw away
that unwieldy decimal
from the start.

Even with smoother
numbers, even canceling
from the population
divisor all willfully
illiterate; un-willfully mute;
those who through
entire lifetimes claim
their fifth amendment;

All those who
said they would
never never never
speak to me
again; those who
had nothing to
say anyway; those
who would let
me starve for
lack of one
precious promissory syllable,

dream answers proved
inaccurate; not even
close, but persisted
through breakfast sequiturs.

Like "Who gets
what?" "A Lottery?"
"Could one sell?"
"Could we swap?"

It delights me
when you smile
at my nonsense,
but, absurdities aside,
I know that
I would give
my three to
you, then mime:

Here, Run, Hide
I will steal
others; bring new
ones daily for
you to say

While I listen
to such music;
while I dance.

To the Pote Who Writes Pomes
(a self-introduction)

Hey, friend,
if it is a pome you are writing
you are not ready yet.

You abuse the Muse; she answers to her name—
a queen who would never respond to *hey you,*
you over there.

You need to know how regal this queen; be ready
to bow, but she and you have not yet been introduced;
her relatives the *Poesies*
and *Poetics*;
some of the *Prosodies*
distant cousins.

In order not to insult, know about them in advance.
A dictionary will help, or maybe an eccentric former composition
teacher. If unavailable, look for someone the age of your
grandmother, who still wears her hair in a bun, and bruises
easily. Her speech perhaps archaic, but bluntly pronounced.

She might tell you of planting *pomes*, hoping they would be firm
for slaw by fourth of July. She might ask you if you can *pote*
some onions in the garden for her. She will thank you for your
potentiation.

I think after this you might write a poem.
But always be careful.
The words have their integrity,
and will not do your work for you,
no matter how you *pote*.

The Dahlia Man

said that day those years ago
he had rather tell me about his apple trees;
no matter how careful you were
something coming from the past could remain secret
about dahlias, something you couldn't always
control and

besides he wouldn't sell me a dahlia
anyway—I wanted tightly fringed
purple ones—he said I had too many children.

Unfairly accused, I explained three belonged
to Tom and India over in Nacoochee across Unicoi
most likely he knew them.

Still too many he said, subtracting.
Dahlias need attention.
Come back in a few years and we'll see.

He said but would you like to hear about my apples?
Said I wasn't going to believe it; said it was God's
truth he had tried to make two hundred and fifty
grafts and only a single solitary one took.

He was right, I didn't believe it—those odds?
Still there they are legible in my notes
of that surreal exchange.

The dahlia man said he had gone
dead twigs in hand
to the living one to figure what in tarnation
could have been right once, just once.

Finally reasoned he said
diameters of both pieces had to be exact
cuts at absolute identical slant
done with a sharp—mind you sharp—knife;
no tearing.
Said sap had to make that leap, get up momentum
for flowing across the dangerous bridge out;

the add-on had to keep pulsing to staunch
too much downflow—if there wasn't the same amount
of life in them it was like one would bleed to death.

Said as you bandaged the wound you couldn't be too firm
or else it was he said you couldn't be too tender.

I moved away. The dahlia man died
and I never did get the tight fringed purples—
took as fair exchange what he said of interface.

Grafts I make often failing, I suffer rejects
where sounds and thoughts don't come out equal,
where images bleed short of bond, where mind
and heart should fuse but at best produce
terminal knotty galls.

Have learned no matter how healing
the intentions words too tender or too strong
won't match at the cellular level
and they die.

I study the living ones.
Sharpen my knife.

When Raquel Reads

Her voice is chocolate, like chocolate
it wraps the words, the centers
creamy or crisp, she hides under
that thick stream of silk
she will hold the pouring ribbon up
to the end, to the end
she will keep pouring
there is some truth she puts off
to the end, holding it up. she will not
let go of the chocolate stream until
the truth she is covering is wrapped
until the covering is so heavy it slides away
and there at the end when the chocolate
is exhausted, the brittle truth is there naked
the truth is so naked and the taste
of the center and the chocolate
is balanced at the end, enmeshed
the truth and the voice and we want
the voice to keep telling us, wrapping
her truths and forget that chocolate
in aftertaste is so bitter, so bitter the aftertaste
the truth has to be paid for by something
we have to pay something
for having that truth
and chocolate a better coating than many
and we have a charge account
and ask her to please read that poem one more time.

A Cowboy Teaches Creative Writing

Some days he even wears boots
and fairly lopes as he enters the room,
hunches across desk, forward,
testing the saddle, then backward, as far
as regimental straight back chair
will tilt, balances, and we know
he will not be easily unseated.

Authority as smoothly camouflaged
as the cowboy's dangling rope
before it lances the air against a target
not yet on the coordinate axis,
knowing X from long experience
almost as surely Y, he moves
to prevent dangerous jockeying
as much as to urge forward
a herd often rambunctious.

With a slight leaning he holds in check
the bulls that scrape horns in narrow places,
swerving from self-hurt
threatening to gore the weaker.

Like the herder, he cuts through,
gentles the cows, the yearlings.
Knowing the narrows ahead
where panic would destroy them all,
he manages with a word, a confiding
mosey beside weak and strong alike,
one by one, to mainstream in order,
and they flow, calmed into open country
where the once dangerous bulls
from far edges watch the sweet grazing.

By semester end, the spurs are gone,
lariat itself abandoned. Now he rides bareback,
comfortable. We too tilt our chairs, lean back,
smell corral.
We swagger. We will all arrive.

Show and Tell

They have brought their treasures
for Show and Tell; as divergent as then second grade
Blondie's recipes written on construction paper
in her made at home binding; then the would-be cynic,
self avowed sarcastic, polishes dog tags as he talks of his grandfather's
odyssey for his son's redemption. Another holds a skeleton key,
guaranteed in fifth grade to open a grandmother's house…
no questions asked, now symbol, he says, of open future.

Then Wes takes from a shelf the Underwood Portable Typewriter,
his grandmother's dearest relic, her name boldly proclaimed on the cover,
now tired and worn as the sluggish keys.

And last, Jason, archetypical Argonaut
tells of his first journey outward, holding the horse urine
marker that would bond the Bremen High School class
who went that time to Charleston, swearing they
would never forget, but now, two years later,
he has not called a one
to say hello.

And what can I say
of their unifying motifs,
these college students in creative writing class?

That they are each of them
at twenty-twenty one
vulnerable to fatal forgetting
but for now, ripe with remembering
and tender to the core.

Silences

Words, saying all
they can
still come short
of all
that silence discloses—

and silence says nothing
until words
are exhausted

then, oh then,
how silence sings.

"What see ye?" comes the call,
certainly not from the past
for he has answered it ever and again,
from the future, not yet.
It be still forming around lips to be called anon.
The future lies before him rolling in the wind.
Behind past, or future for another such as he.

"What see ye?" cries the present.
With flashing smile and reaching arm,
he lifts his voice to the receding call,
"Land ho, off to port quarter, we are home!"

From *Time And The Sea*,
in HINGES AND OTHER MUSINGS,
E. J. Banke, 2006

VIII. Home Free

Parsing

"Gold is where you find it," they have always said.
Such certainty begs other premises
parsed from life's existential grammar.

Music will be when you hear it.
How you feel it is church.
Love is the always and only because.

Anywhich newborn baby soever at all
is the who of hope.

Life is while,
and what is to do is to dance
to home, offered as predicate nominative
for gold where you found it to go back to.

Constant I

When childhood's myths bred credence from despair
and tales of Fancy's early planting grew
to breed a faith in braver saints to dare
to intervene for me, I could subdue
all fears by virtue of a medal worn.
A happy hope foresaw the good in all,
and fairer from the fair was daily born.
But older now, and now no longer thrall,
for time has been to look abroad the land
to find that birds do die of wounded wings;
no strong saint's clasp upon the vagrant's hand;
and everywhere are lutes with broken strings.

Yet, one creed rests, how strangely grown more sure:
Your love remembered still my Christopher.

Apprentice to the First Born

All the voyages, journeys you have taken
or will take, where I could never have gone,
or will go, chartered by circumstance of time,
place, and whatever other companions,
call out to me to say:

Oh, remember our first perilous crossing
alone, alone, and you my only astronomy.
Your pulsar sounding dark treacherous
waters, insisting harbor lay one degree leeward
of pain and fear.

Incredibly it was so.
You were delivered.
I was born.

New Baby

Words smile their way into being.
Diminutives, superlatives, exponentials.
Such newness demands
never before heard language
and we say baby words,
baby, baby language
for you and me to hear.

First Grandson Talks

When Ben talks, (I'm told)
he speaks pronouncements bold.
A Buddha sits on table throne
passing thoughts to be well known.
Syllables rush; cadences clear...
How is it we just barely miss
the gist of his idea?

Ben on arm outdoors
incants on leaf and limb
in language made for grass and flowers
exclusively by him.

In gestures, frowns, and smiles
his body language is precise;
obviously what he says beguiles—
Such excellent advice!

When Ben talks, (I'm told)
he makes warming what was cold,
makes softening what was hard.
Makes rest easy who were tired.
I believe what I am told.
Ben's language
alphabet gold.

Explaining to Leah Simone

Leah, this morning
the snake was coiled so cold,
so just out of its winter birth-place hidey-hole
that it looked like the shell of a giant slug.

It resembled also those sweet buns that curl
from a nice soft bottom
up to a crunchy cinnamoned nut.

You do not know anything about any of this;
snake, sweet roll, or things
that are not what they seem.

That, dear Leah, is why I must tell you
while there is still time.
I lack six months of being eighty-four years old;
you are eight months into our lives.

I had to touch this snake several times with a small stick
to make it move at all; conservation of heat and space
being in its favor. However, I, your great grandmother,
who quit killing almost anything at all when I was thirty five,
quickly killed it when I saw its copper head;
shining and beautiful, yes, but poisonous,
in a home near where your first steps might lead you.

At thirty five a deep grief taught me
that all anything has completely in common
with anything else, including, dear Leah,
though others may dispute it,
the flecks of mica, the granite outcrops,
small pebbles of any sort,
is its own, very own life.

I am deeply conscious
that you and I are linked in that way.

So, what happened that something would change
after forty-eight years
of co-existence with the local snakes,
bears, the ticks, flies, mosquitoes?

YOU happened, Leah,
and innocence carries risk.

Cary at the Piano

I thought the walk had ended before supper.
Her stated aim of gathering nuts
she soon abandoned, though a few,
along with one delicately nibbled dogwood berry,
three specks of mica from the spring
and a single cinquefoil bud rested together
briefly in the basket she made at Out-Of-Doors Camp.

Her focus shifted to snatching falling leaves...
leaves caught arm high, jumped for,
or stolen-base leaves, dived and slid for, held
triumphantly for stripped trees to witness.

She declined my offer of perfect maple
and sweet gum leaves fresh fallen to forest floor.
"I am now filling this basket only with things
that have never touched the ground."

After supper, from bed, I hear her live
the walk at the piano. A hesitant melodic invention
copies the voice of her oblique invitation.

"I am going to the woods—there are such *huge*
acorns there—you really should see them."

Then a surer motif, acorns, all ground things
forgotten in the same way in which she emptied
her basket for the real joys. Her hands flutter
leaves from the high treble, hesitate, fluctuate,
swirl them again upward in memory of wind
from the steep side of Hamby Mountain.

As notes plunge toward earth horizon, left hand
tosses hard, high, intent at least on Middle C compromise.
Over and over keys change, rhythms alter

keeping color and form afloat. Melodies chase
each other, counterpoint checks free fall.

Twilight dampens wind. The walk ends
and her improvisations, with two perfect chords
balance perfectly the basket full
of something that has never touched the ground.

Camping with Delbert, Age 12

He is waiting at the bridge
that begins our farm road,
ready as he said he would be,
outfitted for camping overnight.

He has my things too. Just for me
the sugar. He takes his oatmeal,
like his coffee, black.
Thus rationed sugar and coffee
speckle against waxed paper folds
sized for back jeans pockets.

An aluminum pan, bruised from sitting
on too many stones ringing too many fires
hangs from raveling baling twine tied to his belt.

Four cups, pewtered like the pan handle, nest,
balance his belt-load side to side.
Oatmeal and spoons fill jacket pockets.

Blankets all each must carry, I fold mine
over arms in front. It feels good…
scratches just enough to speak of wool
against cooler night air.

"Wool sheds rain pretty good, too,"
his twelve year old knowledge declares.
"It might rain, but I think not much more
than a sprinkle."

We cross two pastures,
stooping between barbed strands of wire,
taking turns; proud to do it without touching
a single awful knot.

We come to the last of our land
beyond criss-crossing creeks
where laurel and rhododendron
fill the water twice.

For supper we gather blackberries,
the first drupes perfect.

He builds a fire, casual to do it with one match,
and it will watch over our sleeping,
warning away cows whose territory we have borrowed.

It does rain, so lightly that coals
are vibrant under morning ashes.
Oatmeal boils quickly in creek water.
He chooses a Jersey
from among the curious herd,
milks two cups full,
pats her flank to dismiss her for delicate grazing.

The morning is filled with delicious promises.
Delicious and smooth as warm oatmeal.
He has been right about it all. Everything,
every single thing came out even. He took
his coffee black; mine laced with creamy milk,
the sugar just enough,
down to the last grain shaken from waxed paper
which he folds again and puts into his pocket,
while I try to fold everything into a memory,
knowing there is not enough room.

Ginna

Ginna's astronomy at ten
allowed her to command
planetary orbits to linger
by looking out back-yard tent
and pointing her finger.

She moves at plus-thirty
under broader skies
names each discovery
from galaxies
in her lover's eyes.

Lineage

Having no paper, my father
drew birds on soft pine firewood
scavenged from a planer mill.

My granddaughter paints stone
on expensive canvas,
obsessed by granite
as he by feather.

He died, I think of too much making-do,
thirty years before she was born.

I who paint neither bird
nor stone,
love them equally,
backward, forward,
ponder connections.

I having heard stones sing;
having seen birds fall.

Transplanting with Mitsuko

Surely,
there are vast reaches of earth
where my shovel would not encounter stone,
go smoothly at precise angle,
dig away prescribed twelve inch cube,
work removed soil to softness
for this yellow rose.

Somewhere, where alluvial silt
from many floods
has stored nothing but grain
by grain
of loam, ready for easy bedding.

But it is not here.
Not here
where only sprinkles of earth
connect between gneiss
and quartz.

Not here where my daughter
and I learn after rock removal
there is not enough soil to tamp around roots:
how instead, rocks too
must be replaced in volume
by tablespoons of borrowed
composting materials scraped
from under other plants,
they too looking hungry.

The whole procedure
a déjà-vu of personal roots;
how they have fingered
insistently downward,
grubbing nutrient
from something in final analysis
as contradictory, as needful, as rock.

From the Daguerreotype

You look at us serenely
over the years. At eight, your eyes
sober, plump hands composed.
Your braids are perfection;
their gentled tendrils smooth
as velvet bandings at your throat,
your wrists, speaking with rich
folds and tucks someone's special
caring, and you all motherless.
Oh Mother, I send my great mothering love
backwards, to you, aged eight.

At the Breakfast Table

From what out of respect for his geography
I call the south end of the table, long, wide,
too big for just two, still too crowded
when the children come home,
he points with spoon
toward north, to where in summertime
if he were not blind, he could see the blue/green trough
of river and hills up to what is Unicoi Gap,
and speaks of the peneplain.

"I just keep wondering," he says, "how high
that plain must have been, to have smoothed
over the tops of Tray, Unicoi, Yonah, and all around
and in between. The Gap at Unicoi deep,
at least a thousand feet to where the river runs
at some sort of ground zero."

"If I had known when I was a kid, or just older,
what I know now of the geology, hydrology,
I would go looking for microscopic pebbles
in secret caches in the coves. Not moraines
piled by glaciers,
but river and rain-worn-by-centuries rocks
of many natures."

Caught in his dream, I drift also,
long to go gather handfuls
for him to finger. They have to be there,
in creek-sheds, in narrow branches,
tiny veins of the river at deepest bed
of the Chattahoochee,
forever carrying peneplain
until every mountain is laid low.

The coffee is gone: our cups cool,
but we cannot turn away from looking north,
there from the south end of the too-big table.

Let's

I have invited the snow: No
I have entreated the snow
but begged that it come only over the low
pasture and scantily to us higher here,
where our hemlock will hover
over any animal of the wood
that might be lost from nest or food.

And let's you have already milked
and I already have strained, and set the jars
for cream to rise. Let your old air-force jacket
be steaming on the hook nearest the fire.

Let me already have a good bed of coals
and let there be enough smoke to say to those friends,
yes, yes, they are at home; see there is a fire.
And let them now and then look backward
toward their hill opposite, hunch their shoulders usward,
call halloos as they find familiar stones under their feet
and us answering.

And let's say of course you will stay for supper,
and they say of course,
and the kitchen will immediately smell so good
for they have brought new air, and red oak new thrown on fire.

And let's just talk the easy talk of weather and what the children
have been doing, and marvel at how we are never out of things
to talk about. Let's each one have time for a favorite story.
It will not matter that it has been told several times.
We will tell it again, for the snow outside might want to listen.

And as twilight settles let's agree that they will spend the night;
bricks already on the hearth, for warming foot of beds, quilts piled thick.

And then as house things go silent, so will we each and all
and drowsily murmur our good night
and fall asleep to dream
whispers of white falling on white.

Journey

There is a road that I would follow;
a line of sky I need to see
where moon, for sun, lights mountain rim
until sun defines each edging tree.

Agreement made between the two
that light shall mark the valley's edge
and dark be never made complete.
A careful balance kept in pledge

Against the time when mortal eye
has lost all need of sun and sky,
and mountains shrug into the dark
and leave no line to measure heaven by.

Now Children,

It takes a thousand years
or so
to grow an inch
of soil
from all our compacted detritus
compost
whatever we have lost
leaves thrown
to fire
artifacts we drown
in river
sea.

Nothing speeds it much;
we only delay
with concrete
chemical
lead
withholding our dead.

Listen then:

Plant me narrowly
let me sparrowly
marrowly
lie under some tree.

And if I rise
let it be tree
that pumps through death
what it cleans from me
on deep-drawn breath
to gasping skies.

Looking From Dahlonega

The fourth mountain
under the moon—
That one
counting straight down
from where light
spills—
Follow the drip
past silver splatter
on ocean of trees
gone blue,
down to darker
line, again
to the thin shadow,
barely distinct,
limned so scantily,
saying how narrow,
narrow
the valley it shields,

and the next one
just below—

Yes, you see it now—
the fourth one?

That's home.

Whatever of a Holy Spirit

Whatever of a holy spirit in me dwells
is tied by this my body to the earth
so that beneath, the centered cells
that push again toward heaven
make war in vertical degree:
heaven, earth, and me.

Good, evil, and indifference
come close to touching, fail and pass;
approach, and fail, and pass again
as atoms in chaotic mass,
isolates until I lie all lateral,
my battles rendered neutral
by dissolving rain.

Global Warming

There is but one language.
Without words, it smiles.
One music only: the wind.
One river: the dew.
One forest: a tree.
One race:
The newborn child.

Ancestral Ax

Lying there among shells spent
last fall against the deer and pheasant
today I found your ax out in the field.

Coming at day's end, its yield
was more than artifact. It sent
me through lost forests in my mind
to look for you, to see you working there,
but more than that to understand your find:
the dream before the fact.

How did you conceive the blade?
Contrive a shaft? Seeing all you had
was stone, and stick, and vine, what craft?—
far more than cunning—what desire
for strength beyond your hand
led you to find that stone is shaped by stone,
as thought would hone on thought
to shape new man?

I search with visceral pain to know you then,
string history like beads
though on a broken thread.
See you, know you making more than ax;
call you more than friend:
Cry: "I love you, Father,
Millennia dead."

Margery Daw

See-Saw, Margery Daw,
teeter-totter all.
Past and Future players,
each in turn will fall.

Time that was tomorrow
only yesterday
tallies each old sorrow,
starts fresh game to play.

Past grows heavy, future flies
to rim of sky,
holds on tightly, still it slides
down present fulcrum by and by.

So it goes from Greenwich night,
from moments to eternity.
Down to up and up to down,
that's all you have of certainty.

Fly high, Margery Daw,
future's constant lover;
relish present as you slide through,
but it's already over.

Children of Mine

C.B.

Rest easy, first
born,
life is exciting enough
taken in small doses.

The first born always
teaches more than it learns
since it is responsible for three.

DELBERT

Teller of tales
maker of jokes on jokes
breaker and creator of stereotypes
flaunter of all values not personal
you ride a dangerous river in a one-man boat.

Did you hear my
Bon Voyage?

MISSY

Missy, Missy, Missy
          Missy, Missy, Missy,
                    Always, always
                              Herself
                                        Missy.

We forgive life for not
showing us the well where
you draw your joy, since
you brought us so much
of its water.

MITSUKO

"A rose by any other name
Would smell as sweet."
Living proof, our Margaret,
Our Mitsuko, Our Pete.'

Had I known a name that
could have named your
gentleness, I would have
called you that. It is
well, I suppose, that
life keeps secrets.

TERESSA

Teeeeeresssa!
  Contesssssssa!
    Successssssssa!
      Subtle Confessor!

Smiling Teressa!

The last born has to finish
the first born's job.
Consolidate truths.
Take Care of all Pets.
Become parent to parents.
Be adored.

Gone Dancing

Hey,
watch out
when I dance.

When I dance
from the inside
my dance will begin
with an earth-on-axis whirling
everything centered
spinning like mad.

At first I may look like a kite
before my arms become blurred
and disappear out there
as I dance right through fingers
right through tight skin everywhere.

Up, up on toes, I will be taller
than I have ever been;
every thing gone north and south.

Let me tell you,
it will be good
reaching that high
after touching so low.

You may look out and say
there's a whirlwind out yonder!

When already it was likely me
blowing your hat off
as I danced right by you.

Right by you!
and that's no whirlwind out yonder
kiddos, that's me,
your mama
gone dancing.

AFTERWORD

My Beloveds, I Have Written Your Names

giving them to sea and sky
as large as this stick and I can sculpt them
from low tide up to the high berm,
embryo sand castings, letters
gouging ghost shrimp burrows deeply, unevenly.

I disregarded coral skeins, cats' eyes,
fortunes in sand dollars to make
a mile long reading lesson for gulls;
trenches for crab battles,
deceptive cul-de-sacs in ornamented upper case.

In the long view this writing as permanent
memorial as any; no more fragile connection
with your respective memories or dreams
than stone, whose dissolved parent sands
I engraved here.

The short meantime is for wonder.
Will subtle re-arrangements of sand strata
forever declare your names backward,
upside down to the earth's center?

Will turtle or tern erase
with crusty plate or feather
before the moon
traces them through dune shadow
for the night birds to read?

My writing here almost violent,
investing a lifetime of energies
directed at loving you, I pray now
that whatever takes them
will be quiet…

Perhaps froth…
salt grey unsubstantial essence
of what is hardly air, hardly water
whose bondings
as they grip the shallowing troughs
deplete further…
                    and further…

Finally implode
                    Braille-reading your names.

Marsala

The dream came of that sixth year of my life
and memories from the only family reunion I am sure of.
They replay the way we children fought to sit by you
on the bottom step at our grandfather's house
where we gathered for the memorial photograph.

And how going for you in the little Ford car
that had a rumble seat: the front reserved for you,
brought on a battle pure and simple. Who were you?
"This is Aunt Marsala," we were told.
And you? *"This is Sally Mae's child."*

When I was twelve and sent to live there,
you were dead...graduated as a stage-set piece
in family stories. A myth wearing your broad brimmed
white hat, and me victorious beside you on the steps.

How sad that I did not pay more attention.
Even if I might not have understood the affinity
between black Aunt Marsala and my mother.
You keeping alive a blonde baby at your breast.
Your only baby newly dead.

In my mind I go back to that beach
to put your name—not vertically from berm
to low tide, as the others, but over-arching
so that it spans all the spaces from which the others descend.
Pendant, all of us...ours, and theirs to come, and theirs;
you being our Mother's second Mother, Marsala,
saving her for us.

Biography

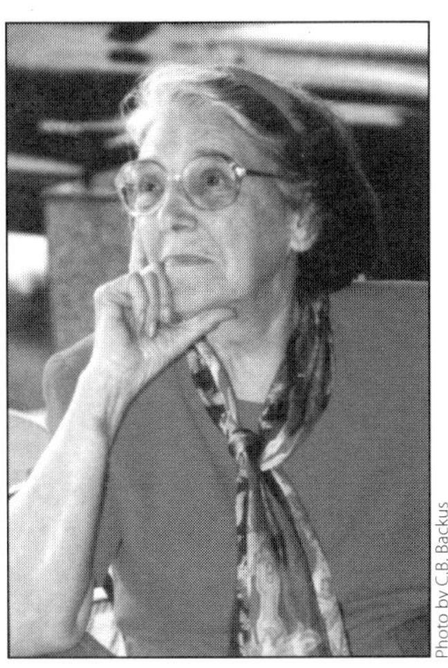

MILDRED GREEAR wrote small poems from the earliest years of her life. Her career goals always were to be a teacher and writer. These she achieved after graduating from Jones Junior College and the University of Mississippi and teaching in Gulfport where she met her husband Philip Greear. At the end of World War II, she moved to the Northeast Georgia mountains where she continued teaching, and became a newspaper columnist, celebrating the rural life of children and chicken farming. Her poetry was not widely shared until after her retirement from teaching in the public schools of Floyd County, Georgia. Her first chapbook submission, *A Species of Ruin*, took first place in the Georgia State Poetry Society contest, and after that, she was published in a variety of regional and international journals. Her second chapbook, *At the Edge*, was also awarded the Charles B. Dickson honor by the Georgia Poetry Society, and she is the only author to twice receive that award.

She has a deep attachment for the remaining Appalachian ethos of her adopted home in White County, Georgia, and along with her family members is an environmental activist.

Thankful for lessons learned from the exigencies of a Depression-era childhood, Greear is fierce in her love of family, the earth, and its diverse peoples. "I learned early how to make a decent biscuit, and from a neighbor that if you have only one egg and five children to feed, you scramble it into gravy. In short, nothing is so small that it cannot be shared, and there are always enough words for poems."

Names Written in Sand

Sally Mae Britt — Burrell Lindsey White, Sr.

Elise Templeton White Cleveland
    Lindsey Britt Moore

Burrell Lindsey White, Jr.
    Lindsey George White

Francis Marion White
    Edythe Frances White McMurry
    Rebecca Marie White Daniels Ritch
    Virginia White Yarbrough
    Judith Faye White Wimberly Ginn
    David Neil White, Sr.

Mildred White Greear
    Carol Britt Greear Carstarphen Backus
    Delbert Philip Thomas Greear
    Virginia Katherine "Missy" Greear
    Margaret Fields Greear Oren
    Teressa Templeton Greear Holtzclaw

Alva Thomas White, Sr.
    Deborah Susan White Johnston
    Alva Thomas White, Jr.
    Alexandra White Rappenacker